+21

THIS BOOK SHOULD BE RETURNED ON OR BEFORE THE LATEST
DATE SHOWN TO ANY LANCASHIRE COUNTY LIBRARY

AUTHOR

HINDLE, D.

CLASS

C091

TITLE BIRDWATCHING WALKS
IN BOWLAND

D1426114

Lancashire
County Council

LANCASHIRE
COUNTY LIBRARY
Bowran Street
PRESTON PR1 2UX
LL1   Recycled

Bowland
Farm

C. Dodding.

Birdwatching Walks in Bowland

by David Hindle and John Wilson, BEM
Art work by Christine Dodding and Nichola Breaks
Maps by Christine Dodding
Colour photographs by Stan Craig ARPS

Royalties to RSPB Birds of Bowland Project
and Lancaster and District Birdwatching Society

Colour reference section funded by

FOREST OF
BOWLAND
Area of Outstanding Natural Beauty

Palatine Books

Copyright © David Hindle and John Wilson, 2005

First published in the UK in 2005 by
Palatine Books
an imprint of Carnegie Publishing Ltd,
Carnegie House,
Chatsworth Road,
Lancaster LA1 4SL
www.carnegiepublishing.com

All *rights reserved*
Unauthorised duplication contravenes existing laws

Cataloguing-in-Publication data
A catalogue record for this book is available from the British Library

ISBN 1-874181-29-2
EAN 978-1-874181-29-3

Typeset by Carnegie Publishing Ltd
Printed and bound in the UK Biddles Ltd, King's Lynn

Disclaimer

The authors have walked and researched the routes for the purpose of this guide. Whilst every effort has been made to represent the routes accurately, neither the authors nor the publisher can accept any responsibility in connection with any trespass, loss or injury arising from the use of the definitive route or any associated route. Changes may occur in the landscape which may affect the information in this book and the authors and publisher would very much welcome notification of any such changes. That said, we sincerely hope that the walks provide many hours of enjoyable birdwatching.

Contents

Foreword

I was delighted to be given the opportunity of previewing *Birdwatching Walks in Bowland* and offering a short foreword. I have a deep-rooted attachment to Bowland; that nook of Lancashire which survived much of the industrialisation of Victorian England. Bowland is still something of a secret and very much a jewel of the North of England.

I have lived at Leagram Hall, Chipping, in the heart of the Bowland Forest since 1965, when my father rebuilt a home on the site of that of my ancestor, the eminent nineteenth-century naturalist, John Weld. He died in 1888 but the changes to our wildlife in the 77 years between his day and ours have been radical.

The biodiversity of Bowland, both on the fells and lowland, is quite wonderful and far greater than just the most obvious visual – birds, mammals and man. We need also to look to their food sources: the trees and shrubs, the wildflowers and grasses, the reptiles and amphibians, fish and molluscs, moths, butterflies and bats. All these species have been affected by our perceived need to grow more food for our ever-expanding towns and cities. We cannot stand back and wait, we have to take decisive action to conserve what is left and even bring back that which is almost lost to our countryside.

Here are some interesting observations recorded by John Weld (1813–88) in his ornithological notes:

Lapwing: 'very common here with many hundreds of eggs taken for the table every year from the end of March to the middle of May.'

Curlew: 'a nest was taken this year 1879 by a Chipping boy at Longridge Fell it had three eggs for which he obtained three pence each.'

Common snipe: 'very common in this part of the country in Spring and Summer leaving us in the first wild weather of September. They breed and have many nests annually in the rushy and ill-drained land. 137 birds were shot on the Leagram range in 1885.'

Corncrake: 'common every year with nests in every meadow. They arrive early in May and leave before the middle of September. A nest containing twelve eggs found in the Hall Meadow in 1884.'

Tragically, the corncrake (amongst others) is now virtually extinct from mainland England and the snipe is in freefall decline.

There are many opportunities now for farmers and land managers, the custodians of our wonderful inheritance, to put something back so that our children and future generations will never have to say 'I remember once hearing the shrill call of the plover and seeing its aerial acrobatic display'.

There are many positive steps being taken in Bowland. A lot of people are doing a great deal of work to conserve and reinstate traditional feeding and breeding grounds. One of the walks described in this book guides the reader along the edge of the Leagram Moss at Chipping. The Moss is a one hundred-acre site which is, with the help of the Countryside Stewardship Scheme and the RSPB, currently being 'improved' for the benefit of wading birds, nesting and feeding.

By raising the water levels, and reducing the heavy overburden of rush, both mechanically and by grazing with traditional and rare breeds of cattle, we now have an oasis in the relatively intensively farmed valley floor. To illustrate the benefits, as we conclude the second year of the project, in 2003 there was one breeding pair of lapwing and one pair of snipe. In the breeding season of 2004 there were nine pairs of lapwing and four breeding pairs of snipe.

This book is the culmination of years of research and hard work on a subject which the co-authors, David Hindle and John Wilson, are clearly so knowledgeable and completely passionate about. David is the author of two books on local history, while John, who was the first warden of the famous RSPB Leighton Moss Nature Reserve at Silverdale, is the author of *The Birds of Morecambe Bay*. Both authors are experienced bird-watchers and both thoroughly dedicated to the cause of conservation.

The book is wonderfully brought to life with the photographs of the late Stan Craig and exquisite vignettes and illustrated plans of the walks by Christine Dodding, with additional material by Nicola Breaks.

David and John's book is a reflection of their deep affection for nature. It is a book intended for the keen bird-watcher, but it also enlightens the serious walker about the birds and wildlife of Bowland. Perhaps more importantly, it offers the opportunity for any of us to link a wonderful walk with the nature that lives there.

I share the deep concern of the authors for the long-term preservation of what makes the area of Bowland so unique. Their dedication to this project is illustrated by the fact that all the royalties for this marvellous publication will be donated to the RSPB Bowland Project and the locally based Lancaster and District Birdwatching Society, which undertakes local survey work.

I can only hope that our shared commitment to the wildlife of Bowland will contribute to a sustainable future.

John Weld-Blundell, Leagram Hall, Chipping

Introduction

The Forest of Bowland, including the detached area of Pendle Hill, was designated an Area of Outstanding Natural Beauty (AONB) in 1964, the eleventh largest of 41 AONBs in England and Wales, covering 802 km (300 square miles) of rural Lancashire and North Yorkshire. Its important biological status is reflected in the fact that 13% of Bowland has been designated a Site of Special Scientific Interest (SSSI). An even greater accolade concerns its status as a designated Special Protection Area under the European Birds Directive, as being of national and international importance, especially for its population of birds of prey and breeding waders. Globally, 75% of all the upland heather moorland in the world and 15% of the global resource of blanket bog are to be found in Britain. The importance of Bowland's heather moorlands and associated ecosystems, comprising fragile blanket bogs with botanical treasures such as the lesser twayblade and sphagnum mosses, is therefore considerable.

A search for other treasures of this area, which may still be seen as a microcosm of all that is beautiful in England, reveals plenty of surprises, not exclusively ornithological. These include a rich, mainly upland flora, supporting a wide range of butterflies, amphibians, reptiles and mammals, ranging in size from Britain's smallest, the pygmy shrew, to the shy Sika deer. The area is ideal for anyone wishing to savour the aesthetics of birdwatching while enjoying tranquil lowland pasture, deciduous woodlands, river valleys, reservoirs and, of course, the fells. There is something for everyone in the Forest of Bowland, from walking, cycling and horse riding to shopping, fell walking and even gliding over a land steeped in historical and archaeological diversity.

The perfect introduction to the area is the popular route known to many as the Trough of Bowland. The road through the Trough cuts through the high fells in central Bowland, alongside ancient stands of Scots pines, and crossing the old boundary between Lancashire and Yorkshire at 'Boundary Hill'. Bowland was formerly part of the Old Forest of the North and the Royal Hunting Forest of Lancaster, and was called 'Bolland'. The Norse interpretation is a derivative of 'Bu' (cattle) or Celtic 'Booa', a cow, signifying 'cowland'. Roman roads bisect a land that was once the haunt of wolves, evidenced by names like 'Wolf Fell' and 'Wolfenhall'. Though much of the uplands are still unenclosed, 'enclosure' brought many dry stone walls to the landscape.

In contrast, the hedgerows comprising ancient enclosure (land enclosed before AD 1600) of lowland areas appear more tamed. The tranquil lowlands and isolated gentle summit of Beacon Fell (266m 873ft) contrast with vast tracts of heather-covered peat moorland and the northern grit-stone fells, rising to the summit of 'Ward's Stone' (550m 1839ft). At the south-eastern boundary, the familiar outline of Pendle Hill (557m 1860ft) nestles like a sleeping leviathan, dominating the landscape. The main rivers – Ribble, Lune, Wyre, Brock and Hodder – are in ecological, geomorphologic and visual terms most impressive, with several featured in our walks. Much of the land in the upper Hodder valley is owned by the Queen, who, as the Duke of Lancaster, is said to have a special affection for Bowland. Other major landowners include the Duke of Westminster at Abbeystead and Mallowdale, and United Utilities which presides over an extensive area of Bowland, mainly to protect their water catchment interests.

Birds often live in the most fascinating places and the best of Bowland's walks that follow should appeal to the serious walker as well as the amateur historian. Many visitors to Bowland are like the birds, seasonal spring and summer visitors. This is perfect, since undoubtedly the best time to visit the area for birdwatching is from late March to July, **with summer migrants best located in early May**. The Forest of Bowland is always well worth a visit and on a beautiful, frosty winter's day the pristine, ancient landscape looks magnificent. It is always worth carrying a camera to capture those memorable views. However, as the fells can be quite inhospitable to birds during the winter, many move to the coast, so two of our walks feature Bowland's birds in their winter quarters, nearby on the Lancashire coast.

The fells are epitomised by the hen harrier, depicted on the logo of the Forest of Bowland AONB and one of a small group of rare species specially protected under the provisions of the Wildlife and Countryside Act. **Contravention of the Act invokes serious penalties for any form of wilful disturbance. The precise locations of the sites of rare breeding birds are naturally omitted but special care should be taken to avoid disturbing these species, so our walks avoid the most sensitive areas whilst still offering opportunities to see all Bowland's rarer species. Disturbance of any breeding birds should be avoided.**

The Countryside and Right of Way Act, 2000

The walks described in this book are either public rights of way or have been approved by the land owners. The Countryside and Right of Way Act, 2000, has now received the royal assent and has been implemented in Bowland. Public rights of way are often signed with coloured arrows or way marks and are not affected by the legislation. Below are the salient features of the new legislation that largely supplement the existing rights but also contain other new and important provisions affecting the walker. We aim to clarify matters while advising readers that further information may be obtained from official sources.

The act does not give people the 'right to roam' wherever they want. It allows people to walk on 'access land', which in Bowland means open country like moorland, and 'common land', marked on the new Ordnance Survey Maps and those produced by the Countryside Agency. 'Access land' is indicated by a small access land symbol on the ground and on information boards at main access points. Most activities on foot, such as walking, sightseeing, birdwatching and running are allowed, but excluded are cycling, riding, driving motor vehicles (including motor bikes and quad bikes), although where they are currently allowed there is no change.

Some types of land are excluded from the access rights, even if surrounded by access land. Excepted land includes cultivated land, buildings and any enclosed area immediately around them, together with any land within 20 metres of a house, quarries and other mineral workings, and livestock pens, although existing public rights of way across 'excepted land' can still be used.

Visitors with dogs on access land

Local restrictions are likely to include a ban on dogs in large parts of Bowland newly opened access land.

Where dogs are allowed, however, to avoid disturbing or injuring wildlife and farm animals, or visitors, they must be kept under control and you must adhere to all special restrictions. A fixed lead is required that is no more than 2 metres long whenever there is livestock near, and at all times from 1st March to 31st July, so they do not disturb nesting birds. Dogs may be excluded completely from grouse moors or lambing enclosures by the landowner and specific local restrictions may limit or prohibit access at certain times. Land owners may suspend or restrict access to any areas of access land for up to 28 days each year, excluding public and bank holidays and most weekends. Where restrictions are required for conservation reasons they will be implemented on the advice of English Nature or English Heritage – for example, to safeguard the nesting of rare birds.

Restrictions do not include trained guide dogs, hearing dogs or dogs on the land with the consent of the landowner, nor will what people already do with their dogs by right, permission or custom be restricted. Local signage will indicate any restrictions but you are strongly advised to use the details on the below to get the most up to date information prior to embarking on a walk.

Naturally the country code should be strictly observed. Drop no litter, close all gates, do not damage walls or fences, or in any way disturb stock, avoid all fire risks, particularly on heather moorlands – and remember, it is now unlawful to dig up or pick many species of wild-flowers.

The Countryside Code

Be safe – plan ahead and follow any signs
Leave gates and property as you find them
Protect plants and animals and take your litter home
Keep your dog under close control
Consider other people

We hope that the above has been helpful in clarifying some of the issues concerning the 'right to roam'. For information on open access areas, phone 0845 100 3298, or visit www.countrysideacess.gov.uk. For more information on birding in Lancashire, check the excellent websites at:

www.eastlancashirebirding.net
www.lancasterbirdwatching.org
www.fyldebirdclub.org

Authors' Preface

This book contains over 30 scenic birdwatching walks, encapsulating the diversity of habitat of this Area of Outstanding Natural Beauty. Most walks are ideal for those who wish to escape either alone or with their families to areas off the beaten track. However, this is far more than just a guide to walks and locations; from the beginning, our underlying aim has been to raise awareness of Bowland's precious heritage and nature conservation generally. Therefore there are occasional references to other aspects of natural history and items of general interest and history; for example, Walk 5 is a productive birdwatching walk along the Hodder, and is called the 'Tolkien Trail' because of Stonyhurst's association with the famous author and naturalist.

Throughout the walks we have highlighted all the species likely to be seen on each walk, which necessarily involves some repetition of species, though birding often yields unexpected results and surprises. In the centre of the book is a short reference section featuring further information on typical birds of Bowland and colour photographs.

Each walk is numbered so that it can easily be cross-referenced to a particular species. For example, the ring ouzel may be sought on Walks 1, 3, 4, 5, 15, 24 and 25. A species guide briefly describes former and current status, ecological requirements and, where appropriate, salient points of identification. The main walk descriptions then follow. Walks are categorised as easy, moderate or strenuous and are illustrated by a sketch map to be used in conjunction with the text. We include a vignette of a typical species to be found on the walk, along with the grid reference, approximate mileage and time duration of each walk. We have endeavoured to commence walks with suitable car parking facilities but, where this has not been possible, alternatives are suggested. The nearest toilet and other facilities are also indicated, though picnic lunches are recommended for the longer walks.

Navigation and safety considerations

Specific directions for each walk are italicised in the text. Often the path you follow will be obvious but no reliance can be put on this, or indeed the presence of signs, particularly over open moorland. Always look ahead for stiles and any yellow way-markers or footpath signs (tip – use binoculars) to avoid having to retrace your steps. Occasionally the going will not be easy, particularly after wet weather, so good walking boots should always be worn. All the walks and access provisions have been checked with the Rights of Way Department at Lancashire County Council but you must be aware that the countryside and its features are constantly changing. Although information was as accurate as possible at time of printing the details of walks may change as certain landmarks may disappear or stiles may replace gates or vice versa.

The guide should be used in conjunction with the Ordnance Survey Outdoor Leisure 41, which embraces the Forest of Bowland, and the appropriate smaller scale Ordnance Survey Pathfinder Series, with precise detail to enhance both navigation and enjoyment.

Fell walks indicated by the symbol (**F**) may require navigational skills and the following considerations are essential:

- When exploring upland areas always carry suitable warm clothing, strong boots and waterproofs, plenty of sustenance, first aid kit, mobile phone and a compass.

- Remember that there are many places in Bowland without clear mobile phone signals.

- Avoid the fells if there is a likelihood of mist descending or bad weather, which can apply even on a fine summer's day without warning. Exposure to cold, wet and windy conditions on the moors can be fatal to those inadequately equipped for sudden changes of weather or overtaken by fatigue.

- The times required to complete walks are all approximate and will vary according to factors such as ability, weather stoppages etc.

- Remember to notify someone where you are going and when you expect to return.

Birdwatching hints

An illustrated book on bird identification will prove useful, with many available at most book sellers. A good pair of binoculars in the range of 8 to 10 magnification is essential, a telescope and tripod are desirable. (The specification of a pair of 8 x 30 signifies magnification by eight times with a 30 millimetre objective or big lens but remember – the wider the lens the brighter the view. The services of locally based specialist retailers who give professional advice on optical equipment for birdwatching should be sought whenever possible.) Being aware of the songs and calls of birds is an important aid to their location and identification, particularly with the warblers colloquially known as 'the little brown jobs'. Birdsong can be learned by listening to one of the many tapes or compact discs now available; reinforcement comes from listening to the songs in the field – along with plenty of patience and concentration. Remember that birds also have ears, so a careful, quiet approach will produce better viewing. Aim to blend into the countryside by wearing suitably coloured clothing.

Acknowledgements

It is a pleasure to acknowledge the help given by the following people and organisations in the production of this book: Barbara Craig for supplying the excellent photographs taken by her late husband Stan Craig, ARPS; John Weld-Blundall for kindly writing the foreword; Christine Dodding and Nicola Breaks for their artistry; Garth Sutcliffe for reading and commenting on the final draft. Nick Osborne (Lancashire County Council) for help with rights of way and the right to roam legislation. Susan Conway and the Forest of Bowland AONB for their general support and for helping to fund the colour reference section; and all our other friends and birdwatching acquaintances for supplying information and sightings.

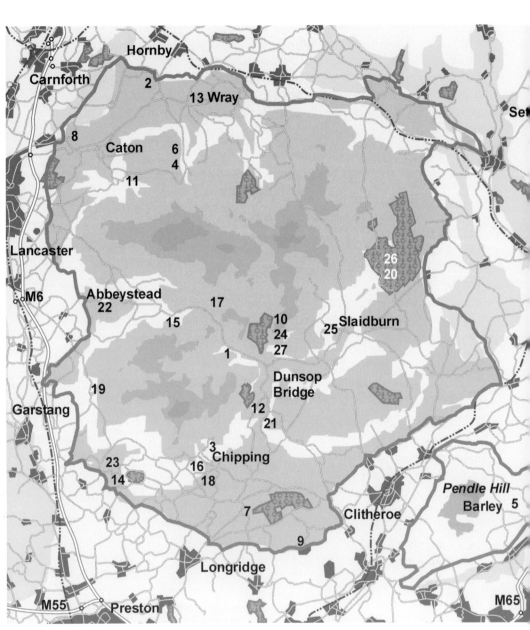

Sketch map of the Bowland AONB. The numbers indicate the approximate start point for each walk. (Walks 27–30 lie beyond this map to the west see walk descriptions.) (*Drawn by* A. Gregory, *Carnegie*)

Quest for the mountain blackbird

Ring ouzel

Start: start and return at the west side of the Trough of Bowland road, south of Syke's Farm

Grid reference: SD 634512

Distance: 6.5km (4 miles)

Time: allow up to 5 hours

Grade: easy

General: nearest public toilets and refreshment facilities are at Dunsop Bridge.

S everal of our walks have a particular theme or something to look out for and here we profile the mountain blackbird or ring ouzel. Our first walk up the beautiful Langden valley encompasses fine wildlife habitat and offers a chance to observe some of the most cherished birds in England, together with a few attractive butterflies, including the green hairstreak. The diverse habitat ranges from open heather moorland, managed for the red grouse, to rocky slopes with scattered small plantations of oak fringing the Langden brook, an attractive stream that flows through the steep-sided valley. The walk describes an easy route to Langden Castle and the return. Do not expect Langden Castle to be an impressive castle of medieval proportions or you will be disappointed on reaching a humble barn with a pretentious-sounding name! Allowing for good birdwatching, the walk will ideally absorb a pleasant spring morning.

1. *Take the footpath indicated 'footpath to Langden Castle and Head of Fiens-dale'. A tree-lined access road leads to the United Utilities Water Works. Continue up the valley.*

Before leaving the car park look up for buzzards and kestrels. At ground level

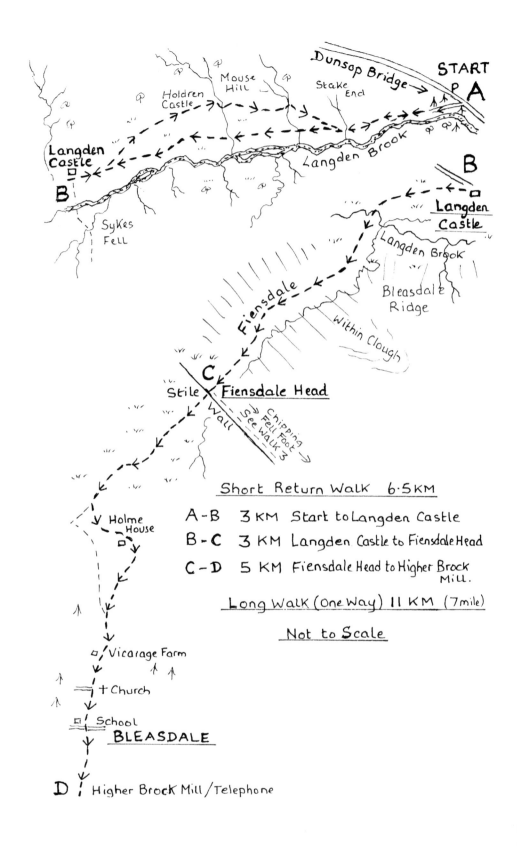

Dunsop Bridge →

START
P A

Mouse Hill

Holdren Castle →

Stake End

Langden Brook

B

Langden Castle

B

Langden Castle

Langden Brook

Sykes Fell

Fiensdale

Bleasdale Ridge

Within Clough

C

Stile × Fiensdale Head

Wall

Chipping Fell Foot → See Walk 3

Short Return Walk 6·5 KM

A–B 3 KM Start to Langden Castle

B–C 3 KM Langden Castle to Fiensdale Head

C–D 5 KM Fiensdale Head to Higher Brock Mill.

Long Walk (One Way) 11 KM (7 mile)

Not to Scale

Holme House

Vicarage Farm

† Church

School

BLEASDALE

D Higher Brock Mill/Telephone

the chaffinches have grown very tame from constant feeding and small flocks invariably frequent the car park. Look out for bird parties busily feeding in the trees, including goldcrests, great spotted woodpeckers, tree creepers, coal tits, long-tailed tits and more familiar blue and great tits. In winter and early spring, before the migrants arrive, the fells are quieter but resident red grouse and stonechat are often present. This can also be a good time to see flocks of crossbills as they fly over the open spaces in their relentless pursuit of cone-bearing trees, sometimes perching on the conifers close to the water works. Flocks of siskin and chaffinches and smaller numbers of lesser redpoll may also be visible in any season, with the robust mistle thrush and tiny wren, currently our most common British bird. In late spring and summer the spotted flycatcher may appear both here and near the waterworks, where the balmy days of summer are characterised by swifts and house martins hawking for insects.

2. *After the Water Works, enter the open valley alongside Langden brook. Stay on the track and keep left at the first junction.*

Reed bunting frequent the rushy areas, teal spring up from the beck and heron pose motionless. Expect to see stonechat, grey and pied wagtails, together with that characteristic Bowland bird, the semi-aquatic dipper. In spring the vocalising tones of the common sandpiper complement its quivering flight along the Langden Beck. The handsome black and white oystercatcher, with its long orange bill, has now taken to nesting on inland rivers and hardly needs an introduction. Listen and watch for the evocative spring flight of the curlew (symbol of wild places like Bowland) which announces its name amongst a fantastic repertoire of calls – sheer joy! At any time of the year red grouse, with their distinctive red wattle, may be seen or heard almost anywhere after leaving the car park, often standing proudly on a favourite tussock, rock or wall like sentinels guarding their domain. Another familiar bird may now herald its presence, for its call is one of the most familiar of all: look and listen out for the cuckoo perched or in flight. This remarkable bird, which inspired great literary figures and composers, is not nearly so common as in the days when Delius orchestrated its famous call as part of his musical score.

3. *The track provides a good vantage point for looking at the rocky slopes and tree lined cloughs to the north.*

In spring the beautiful song of the tree pipits, perching or performing their parachuting display, will help to distinguish them from the very similar, though more abundant, meadow pipit. In spring check the bracken-covered slopes on the south side of the stream as they are a favoured haunt of the whinchat. Simultaneously listen for the metallic alarm call of the nationally declining ring ouzel. If the male is on territory its white crescent usually betrays its presence, perched on a rock or at the top of a small tree while singing its rather melancholy and repetitive song. The female is brown with a narrower and duller crescent and together they add the finishing touches to the valley.

4. *Start the descent to Langden Castle, which may now be seen ahead to the left of the track. The castle represents the end of the shorter described bird-watching walk.*

Linger at Langden Castle for an hour or two, to enjoy raptor watching and some refreshments, in the company of the resident wheatear, with its endearing stance and conspicuous white rump. The presence of birds of prey is often betrayed by carrion crows mobbing them in flight and the largest member of the family, the raven, has only recently expanded its range to Bowland. Ravens may be seen flying high, uttering a distinctive, deep bass bark, 'pruk, pruk', and sporting a distinctive diamond tail. Taking care not to confuse the raven with carrion crows and birds of prey, you may now well have the unique opportunity to spot five species of upland breeding raptors, including merlin, peregrine falcon, buzzard, kestrel and hen harrier. Search the slopes for the handsome slate-grey male hen harrier and brown female. The male may well be engaged in a most memorable tumbling display flight known as 'sky dancing'. Of course, it is a case of 'wait and see', so if possible take the telescope and tripod – it could well be worth it!

5. *Return via an alternative loop to the north of the outward route. After the first ascent, fork left to parallel the lower track, before rejoining ahead of the Water Works, thus gaining further opportunities to observe the valley's characteristic birds from a more elevated viewpoint.*

Walk 1A

Returning via the head of Fiensdale

Distance: 11km (7 miles)
Time: allow 8 hours
Grade: extended walk is strenuous in places
General: no facilities until reaching Chipping.

There is an option to extend the walk at Langden Castle to Fell Foot or Bleadale via Fiensdale Head. If you decide to do the long walk, alternate transport should be arranged at the end.

6. *A detailed Ordnance Survey Map and compass are essential to follow the network of footpaths and access areas, where the relevant Lancashire County by-laws are exhibited. Follow the yellow way-markers up the valley and cross Langden Beck. Continue to follow the way markers along the track that climbs the steep sided valley of Fiensdale onto the wind-swept heather moorland of black peat and boggy terrain, until you reach a stile/fence. At this point you may cross over the stile to descend Holme House Fell past Bleasdale Circle and onto the road at Higher Brock Mill where your telephoned ETA will have assured that waiting car – we hope! Alternatively, to reach 'Fell Foot' or Chipping, follow the route detailed in Walk 3.*

In this upland habitat there is a good chance of seeing the range of birds available on the first part of the circular walk.

The two rivers trail

A walk along the rivers Wenning and Lune

Start: starts and finishes at Hornby Bridge car park
Grid reference: SD 586683
Distance: 5.5km (3.4 miles)
Time: allow 3 to 4 hours
Grade: easy
General: toilets at Bull Beck car park, Caton;
other services in Hornby or Wray.

This pleasant walk besides the rivers Wenning and Lune gives an opportunity to watch all the bird species associated with riverine habitats within the area.

1. *Park in the car park by the Wenning Bridge in Hornby. Cross the river and after pausing on the bridge to look upstream, take the path downstream towards the Lune.*

The breakwater just upstream from the bridge is one of the most regular haunts of dippers and grey wagtail, the tumbling water acting as a magnet to these fast-flowing water birds. Very used to people, they ignore any movement on the bridge. Continue to watch for dippers and grey wagtails, especially on the shingle and exposed rocks, and with them in spring and summer will be common sandpipers. Kingfishers are seen regularly, either fishing from a suitable perch or speeding over the water. Search the fringing trees for woodland birds, including tree creepers and long-tailed tits, and in spring and summer spotted flycatchers. In winter the alders often attract siskin and redpolls.

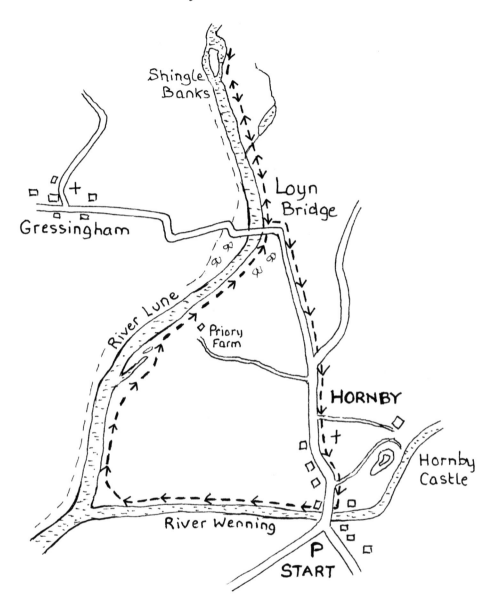

2. *Pause where the trees start to thin to look across the river at the small ox-bow lakes on the south bank of the Wenning.*

These are well used by wildfowl and waders, especially mallard, shelduck, mute swan, lapwing and redshank which breed in the area, while in winter they are joined by flocks of wigeon and teal. Fieldfare and redwing feed in autumn on the hawthorn berries and later in the winter search for worms in the damp pastures, and with them large flocks of lapwing and golden plover can often be found. During passage periods, these fields and pools are frequented by small flocks of meadow pipits and pied wagtails.

3. *Where the two rivers join, stop to scan the shingle beds and river banks.*

Throughout the year the area is alive with birds. During the breeding season there can be found oystercatcher, goosander, redshank, Canada goose, sand martin, curlew, lapwing, kingfisher, and possibly snipe, ringed plover and yellow wagtail. If your visit coincides with spring or autumn passage, you may be lucky and see some of our irregular visitors such as osprey, black tern, little gull, little ringed plover and greenshank. All these and several other species have been recorded passing along the valley, usually staying close to the river. In winter, flocks of lapwing and golden plover frequent the fields and often rest on the shingle banks. Wildfowl include mallard, wigeon, teal, goosander and Canada goose, whilst in late winter they are often joined by a flock of greylag.

4. *Walk upstream along the Lune. The main geological features of the river can be seen – the sand banks over-laid on bands of millstone grit and, of course, the extensive shingle banks.*

The Lune is known for its quick and sudden rise following heavy rain in the catchment, which helps keep the sandy banks suitable for nesting sand martins and kingfishers and keeps the shingle beds clear of vegetation. This stretch attracts pied wagtails and goosander, the latter of which nest in large holes in trees, sometimes at quite a height. When hatched the downy young simply jump out and bounce as they land! From mid-May, broods of goosander are frequent, often linking up with other broods to form a crèche. The males, like most wildfowl, take no part in the parental duties; in fact ringing has shown that many go to Scandinavia to moult. Many oystercatchers nest on the shingle banks, running the risk of being flooded out by high water levels. Others nest in the adjoining fields, where floods are not usually a problem, though the trampling feet of cattle and sheep make raising a brood equally difficult. However, oystercatchers are one of our longest living birds, so they need only occasional good years of productivity.

5. *Follow the obvious track along the river towards the bridge, passing first through scrub and then mature woodland.*

During and just after the breeding season, look out for willow and garden warblers, blackcap, redstart, long-tailed tits and chiffchaff. Nuthatches and great spotted woodpeckers are present throughout the year and buzzards are often seen overhead. The gracefully proportioned seventeenth-century Loyne Bridge comes into view. Skilfully built to take advantage of a rocky outcrop and originally designed to take horse and cart, it now takes single-track modern traffic.

6. *Continue under the bridge, along the bank as far as the first main shingle bed. From there it is necessary to return to Loyne Bridge, from where it is possible to retrace the route back along the river to the car park. Alternatively, make a circular walk on the road back to the car park down the main street of Hornby, passing the hen harrier logo of the AONB as you enter the village.*

The river here currently has two sand martin colonies, although colonies can move from one season to another. Always busy, such colonies offer the best watching during April, when the birds are excavating the half-metre-long holes, the bottom of the cliff face being covered with the newly excavated sand. By late May young are being fed and as they grow the impatient young poke their heads out of the hole, turning to watch every passing bird in the hope of a parental meal. Two broods are reared in most years, although some nests are washed out by floods. Sand martins prefer to nest in steep banks and are very colonial so need a tall, long bank, preferably over water. Kingfishers are not so choosy and will make their nest hole in a small bank or even under the roots of trees. This stretch hosts the same breeding species as section three above.

During spring and summer, house martins, swallows and swifts can be seen over the village and spotted flycatchers in the gardens, whilst in winter a wide range of woodland birds frequent the well-stocked feeders put out by bird lovers. Check again for dippers and grey wagtails from the Wenning bridge.

Birding on the Chipping Fells

Wolf Fell, Langden Castle, Fairsnape and Parlick circular

Hen Harrier.   C.D.

Start: starts and finishes at Chipping
Grid reference: SD 622434
Distance: 20km (12.5 miles)
Time: allow 8–10 hours
Grade: strenuous
General: parking, toilets and refreshment facilities at Chipping.

T his is the hardest of the described walks. It is vital that you are adequately equipped with appropriate clothing and a compass for walking over exposed moors that embraces the summit of Fairsnape (520m 1707ft). The fording of Langden Beck may present a problem when the stream is in spate so take a spare pair of socks. This is not recommended as a family walk for younger children or during winter time when daylight hours are short. Good weather and a good forecast are crucial. To cap it all, the fells were used for military training during World War 11 and you may even come across something that looks like an unexploded shell – do not touch, do not panic, but do inform the police.

In order not to paint too bleak a picture, it is right to point out that on a glorious day, the heather-clad moors present an unfolding vista of spectacular views. The southern outlying Bowland fells of Pendle Hill and Longridge Fell are impressive. The view from Fairsnape of the Lancashire plain extending to the Isle of Man, and the glistening sea between the Cumbrian

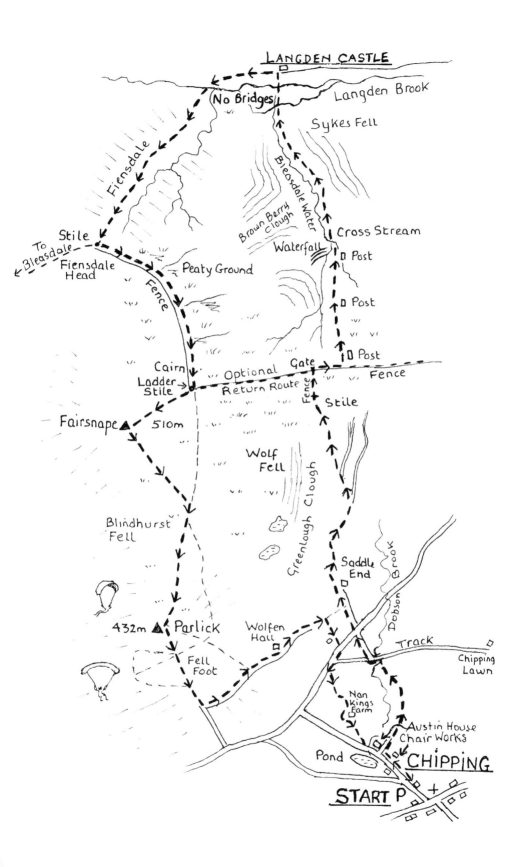

and Welsh Mountains is equally so, not forgetting the familiar landmark of Blackpool Tower.

1. *The route from Chipping to the lower fells at Saddle End farm begins and ends close to the mill lodge at Berry's Chipping Chair Works. Proceed along the road beyond the chair works, past the expanse of water with its motley collection of ducks, to a footpath on the right just before 'Austin House'. Follow yellow way-markers up the rise, before crossing a field and dropping down to a footbridge over Dobson's Brook. Cross over the footbridge and turn left on the farm track to emerge on a metalled road. Take the concrete track directly opposite leading to Saddle End Farm. Walk ahead, keeping left on a well-defined track alongside a wall and continue uphill to a sign indicating 'Saddle Access Area' by a wall stile. At this point the track is well defined but shortly thereafter it divides into a number of grassy path depressions. Interestingly, these tracks were originally made by sledges during rush-gathering for bedding for animals and peat for burning. Keep to the left-hand track, with Greenlough Clough on your left, and proceed uphill to a wire fence with a sign indicating 'Wolf Fell Access Area'. Do not go over the stile onto the access area but follow the fence uphill to a gate/stile. See below for alternative short return route.**

   After the gate the track is poorly defined and if the mist comes down you will need that compass! Go through the gate and turn right along the fence, following it for about 200 metres. Look for a solitary post near the fence and turn left at 90 degrees, heading north-north-west towards the remote clough that harbours Bleadale Water. Follow a few more posts that descend the south and east side of the clough, with its attractive waterfall, to eventually ford Langden Beck. You will need that spare pair of socks while taking a break at Langden Castle.

On the first section of the walk, a melancholy song heard from the tops of trees consisting of a rolling tuee-tuee-tuee with terminal flourish, is useful in locating yet another Bowland gem, the redstart. It is sometimes possible to take advantage of the elevation to look down on singing male redstarts close to Dobson's Brook. On the lower fell sides and in-bye, kestrel, cuckoo, lapwing, curlew, snipe, woodcock, skylark, meadow pipit and stock dove, plus occasional wandering hen harriers, may all be seen during spring and summer.

On the higher bracken and heather-covered slopes look out for whinchat, ring ouzel, and short-eared owl. Soaring or hunting raptors on the hills

---

*   A shorter walk is offered at Wolf Fell by crossing over the stile onto the Wolf Fell Access Area and continuing along an obvious path through the heather, eventually reaching a ladder stile in the top boundary with the Fairsnape Access Area. Rejoin the described walk and follow the directions back to Chipping from the summit of Fairsnape.

should include merlin, sparrow hawk, kestrel, hen harrier, peregrine falcon and buzzard. At Bleadale Water and Langden Castle most of the birds described in Walk 1 are probable, such as common sandpiper, wheatear, stonechat and dipper, so reference should be made to this walk for a more descriptive account of the birds of the Langden Valley.

2. *Follow the yellow way-markers up the valley and again cross Langden Beck. Continue to follow the track that climbs the steep-sided valley of Fiensdale onto the wind-swept heather moorland, comprising black peat and boggy terrain, until you reach a stile/ fence. Here you may cross over the stile to descend Holme House Fell past Bleasdale Circle and onto the road at Higher Brock Mill. However, to reach the starting point at Chipping, our route takes you over the summits of Fairsnape and Parlick Fell. Turn left alongside the fence and follow the fence – crossing over a stile – for about one kilometre to reach the 'Wolf Fell and Fairsnape Access Areas'. Reaching the ladder stile, keep right of the fence and make a slight detour onto the summit of Fairsnape by heading towards the prominent cairn (Paddy's Pole) and trig point. From Fairsnape summit, regain the path to cross over a fence stile and follow a broad track to a wall. Turn right and drop down onto the lip of Blindhurst Fell, following the path alongside a wall. Walk onto the crest connecting Parlick with the main mass, to reach the summit of Parlick. Cross over a stile and descend the steep, south-eastern face of Parlick to Fell Foot.*

From Fell Foot proceed down the lane towards Startifants Lane. Turn left along the drive to Wolfen Hall, turning right onto the footpath by the cattle grid, thus avoiding the hall. Continue along the footpath, following the prominent marker posts and crossing over a footbridge at Chipping Brook. Just before Saddle End Farm, turn right along the footpath towards a small barn surrounded by trees. After the barn, turn right on the metalled road to reach a footpath sign on the left that takes you across pasture and past farm buildings, culminating in a steep descent onto the roadway, just ahead of Berry's Chair Works at Chipping.

In upland habitat there is a good chance of seeing the range of birds to be seen on the first part of the circular walk. In May small trips of dotterel and odd golden plovers have been found on the summits but do not be surprised if you see neither. Conversely, the red grouse is a likely companion throughout the walk, with a few wheatears and meadow pipits usually present.

On more fertile ground on the walk back to Chipping, expect to see any of the following birds: kestrel, sparrow hawk, red-legged partridge, little owl, jackdaw, curlew, lapwing, stock dove, goldfinch, greenfinch, chaffinch, grey wagtail, pied wagtail, skylark, meadow pipit, swallow, swift, blackbird, song thrush, mistle thrush, robin, titmice, willow warbler, blackcap and garden warbler.

The Hornby road

Stock Dove

Start: small informal lay-by just before the bridge over the River Roeburn on the Hornby to High Salter Road*

Grid reference: SD 601639

Distance: 6.5km (4 miles)

Time: allow 3–4 hours

Grade: easy to moderate

General: toilets at Bull Beck car park, Caton; other services in Hornby.

The classic cross-Bowland walk from Roeburndale to Slaidburn cuts through the heart of the hill country. Featured here is the short walk, returning by the outward route. On this scenic walk the bird population changes from those of woodland and farmland, through moorland edge species, to the true moorland specialists. It is well worth recording both the species and numbers seen on the walk. The numbers of species recorded in spring can, with luck and perseverance, approach 70, declining to about 20 in winter.

1. *From the lay-by, pass over the bridge and follow the road towards High Salter Farm.*

Pause on the bridge to check for dipper, grey wagtail and common sandpiper on the fast-flowing river. This is also an excellent place to scan for raptors,

---

* Short and long verions of this walk start here, the short returns but on the long walk to Slaidburn (18 km) appropriate transport arrangements are required – allow 8–10 hours. This walk eventually links up with Walk 25.

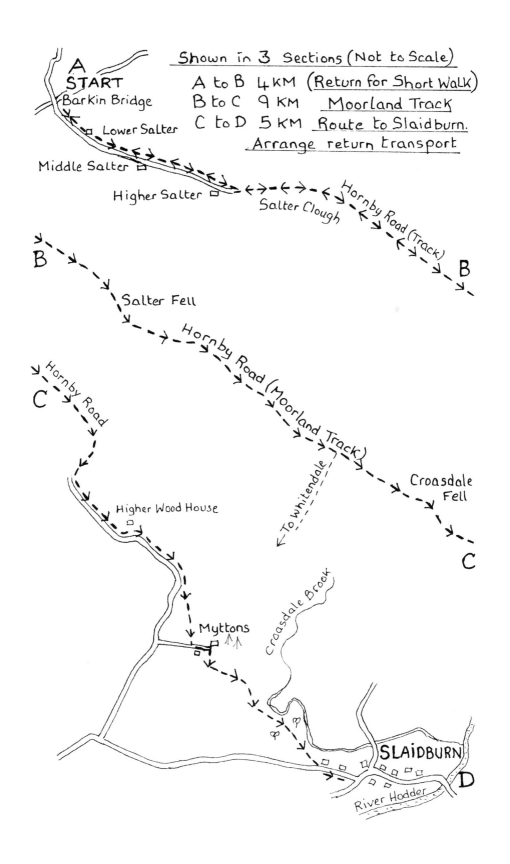

Shown in 3 Sections (Not to Scale)
A to B 4 KM (Return for Short Walk)
B to C 9 KM   Moorland Track
C to D 5 KM   Route to Slaidburn.
Arrange return transport

A
START
Barkin Bridge
Lower Salter
Middle Salter
Higher Salter
Salter Clough
Hornby Road (Track)
B
B
Salter Fell
Hornby Road (Moorland Track)
C
Hornby Road
Higher Wood House
To whitendale
Croasdale Fell
C
Croasdale Brook
Myttons
SLAIDBURN
D
River Hodder

including buzzard, sparrow hawk and kestrel. Little owls are often seen in daylight, perched on the fence posts or walls, both here and along the road from Hornby. The woodland close to the bridge hosts long-tailed tits, tree creepers and other woodland birds, including at times pied flycatchers which breed in several woodlands in the Roeburn valley. Tree pipits sing from the woodland edge or from isolated trees, while cuckoos regularly call, both from perches and on the wing.

2. *The road to High Salter is through pleasant 'in bye' farmland with hedges, walls, scattered trees and woodland patches.*

Many species breed here, including redstart, mistle thrush, goldfinch, linnet, pied wagtail, spotted flycatcher and many woodland species. The recent planting of hedgerows and trees at Lower and Higher Salter will gradually attract more birds. Look out for stock doves which frequent several of the farm buildings, along with swallows and house sparrows. Both redstart and pied wagtail use holes in the stone walls for nesting, whilst away from the silage meadows, skylark and meadow pipits are frequent.

3. *The track now passes through the gate at High Salter, on towards the moorland.*

One is immediately struck by the abundance of breeding waders in many of the rough, rush-dominated grazing fields. From early March to early July the four common species, curlew, lapwing, redshank and snipe, are usually vocal as you approach. The level of calling peaks in early spring as territories are established and females attracted. It subsides somewhat during incubation but reaches its highest intensity when young are about. The exception is the snipe, which is most vocal from late March on into May, with two territorial calls, the first of which is the 'chipper chipper' note, usually delivered while perched on a fence post or wall. The 'drumming' or 'bleating' of the male is a superb sound, best heard on a still morning or evening. One never ceases to wonder that this sound is produced by the stiff outer tail feathers standing out at about 45 degrees and vibrating in the rush of air as the bird shoots down. It is appropriately know locally as the 'heather bleater'. This abundance of breeding waders is a joy and it is this habitat, mostly unaffected by recent agricultural intensification, that makes Bowland one of the most important areas for breeding waders in Britain.

Other breeding species in this area include cuckoo, a few wheatear, many meadow pipits and skylarks. There is a constant movement of both lesser black-backed and herring gulls to and from the colony on Tarnbrook and Mallowdale Fells, as small groups head out to feed on the inter-tidal areas of Morecambe Bay or the urban tips and land fill sites. After the breeding season, flocks of rooks, starlings and meadow pipits frequent these fields.

4. *Follow the track onto the moorland proper. If you are returning to the start, go as far as you like before re-tracing your steps. For those doing the walk to Slaidburn, follow the well-marked track.*

Waders gradually become less common as the habitat becomes more heather-dominated but look out for golden plover, which occur usually in grassy, short heather or bare, eroded patches of peat or burnt areas. They are rather thinly distributed and can be easily overlooked, although the alarm notes of the off-duty bird are usually the first signs of their presence. They share the same habitat with another rare breeding wader, the dunlin, which, partly due to its smaller size, is even more difficult to locate, although again the alarm note and the soaring display flight are good signs. In some areas the dunlin is called the 'plover's page' because of the very close association of these two species. Meadow pipit and, to a lesser extent, skylark, are common breeders. In the past, twite have been recorded breeding but not recently.

Red grouse become common in the heather areas and watch out for both whinchat and stonechat in the valleys, especially where the heather is thick or there are stunted trees and tall bracken. The track is a good vantage point to watch for Bowland's raptor specialities, the hen harrier and merlin. Scanning the heather areas usually produces the best results. Take care not to miss the pale grey male harrier among the large numbers of lesser black-backed and herring gulls, especially when it is quartering the heather at a distance. The much smaller merlin uses its superb turn of speed to fly down its main prey, the abundant meadow pipit. This is also prime habitat for the diurnal hunting short-eared owl, whose population fluctuates, the largest numbers occurring during years when voles are abundant.

Walk 5

Dotterel over Pendle

Dotterel   CD

Start: start and finish at Barley

Grid reference: SD 823404

Distance: 6.5km (4 miles)

Time: allow 4 to 5 hours

Grade: moderate

General: parking, toilet and refreshment facilities at Barley.

Old Demdike, Chattox and Alice Nutter were members of an infamous coven of around ten witches, who, with many of their supposed victims, used to live in the farms and villages around Pendle, prior to their demise on the scaffold at Lancaster Castle in 1612. Pendle is the highest hill in Lancashire and is famous for its witches and for its association with the Quaker movement, for it was in 1652 on Pendle Hill that George Fox had his vision which led to the foundation of the religion. We will not be meeting any 'witches over Pendle' on this walk for nowadays the big end of the hill, which rises to a height of 557m (1860ft), is more famous for 'dotterels over Pendle'. The most productive time for this walk and to coincide with the spring passage migration of small flocks or trips of Dotterel, is the last week in April and the first two weeks in May.

1. *Pendle may be approached from Barley by taking the 'Pendle Way' footpath that leads left off the Barley to Clitheroe road. From the main road, take the footpath towards Pendle House. A triangular walk is marked on the Ordnance Survey Outdoor Leisure 41 with the symbols of recreation/public footpath. It is more productive and less arduous to ascend on the footpath to the left of*

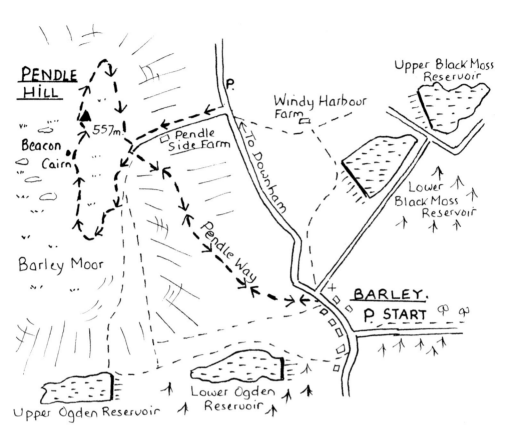

the big end of Pendle and to complete a circular walk by coming down the
stepped recreational path on the northern side.

Look and listen for lapwing, snipe and curlew engaged in their evocative vocal
display flights over the fields. Around the farm buildings, swallows, goldfinch,
house sparrow and pied wagtail are often present. Surprisingly, the scarce
black redstart has been seen in the vicinity of the farmsteads at the foot of
the big end of Pendle.

2. *Commence the ascent of Pendle Hill, taking care to avoid causing erosion by
   keeping to the footpaths.*

Keep an eye on the walls and posts for the whinchat during spring. When
climbing the slopes, chance encounters with ring ouzel are possible during
their April spring passage. The wheatear is a common summer visitor and it
conspicuous white rump usually belies its presence on the slopes, but regret-
tably the twite is now rarely spotted at this former haunt. Nowadays the
stonechat has taken to frequenting such upland areas and may be seen here.

Overhead the kestrel, sparrow hawk, peregrine and raven may be seen throughout the year. Meadow pipits are common on the slopes.

3. *Reaching the Pendle plateau, walk right towards the triangulation point. At the first cairn, veer diagonally left towards an extensive area of rock terrain, recessed below the level of the peat.*

This is the key habitat for trips of dotterel but do not enter this zone until first viewing from a respectable distance with optical equipment. Unnecessary disturbance should be avoided at all costs, in the interests of both the feeding migratory birds and other people seeking the opportunity to see them, as if you cause them to fly they will probably not return. From this habitat of the dotterel, look for a concrete-flagged walk before reaching the triangulation point and take a walk along it before retracing your steps. On the vast upland area of the Pendle plateau cotton grasses, sedges, crowberry, heather and cranberry provide an attractive haunt for a few red grouse. Overhead the skylark ascends ever higher in unstoppable and quintessential melodic flow. The blanket of peat covering Pendle is the haunt of the golden plover, with its plaintive call, symbolising such wild places. Golden plovers are in decline due to afforestation schemes but one or two pairs are usually present during spring and occasionally winter.

A walk to the summit is well worth it in winter when another key species may be sought. Flocks of up to 80 snow buntings are now a significant ornithological feature of Pendle Hill during the period from November to February. Like the dotterel, this large bunting nests in the Cairngorm mountains of Scotland. Look in the longer cotton grass and listen as flocks fly overhead with their pleasant and distinctive rippling/trill calls. Normally snow buntings are seen at lower coastal altitudes but Pendle Hill provides an opportunity to see them in all their splendour in a superb upland setting.

Woodland treasures of Roeburndale

Pied Flycatcher

CD.

Start: start and return to the informal lay-by on the
Hornby High Salter Road
Grid reference: SD 601639
Distance: 5.5 km (3.5 miles)
Time: allow 3–4 hours
Grade: easy to moderate
General: toilets at Bull Beck car park, Caton;
other services in Hornby.

This attractive walk traverses the woodlands and adjacent grasslands of one of Bowland's most interesting valleys. The birds are typical of upland, ancient woodland and include specialities of this attractive habitat. Although an interesting walk at any time of year, it is at its best in spring. This is a recently established conservation walk so will not be found marked on the OS map. It is part of DEFRA's policy of opening up parts of the country-side while delivering a conservation message and has been established with the full support of the four landowners and farmers concerned. DEFRA is to be congratulated on the excellent way marking and provision of stiles, bridges and even steps in difficult situations, making this one of the easiest of walks to follow. The Roeburndale woodland is one of Britain's best and largest examples of an upland, broad-leaved, natural woodland, and is a Site of Special Scientific Interest and a Biological Heritage site, mainly because of its botanical interest.

1. *Cross the stile over the wall and into the field and follow the woodland edge. Because of the steep wooded slope down to the river, one is walking almost at tree top height, mainly looking down into the trees and so giving excellent views of birds in the canopy.*

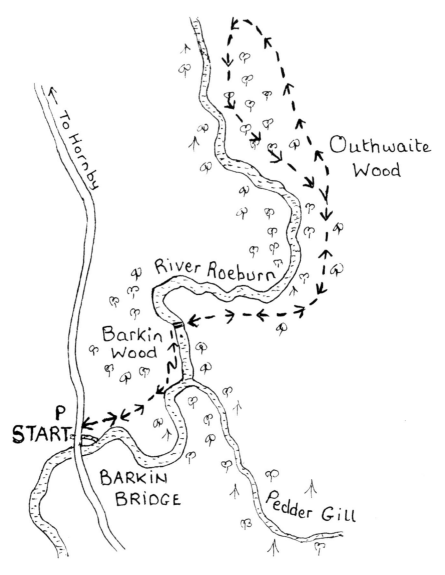

The habitat in parts of this woodland is ideal for the three specialists of upland, mainly oak woodland. Both pied flycatcher and wood warbler prefer mature, sessile, oak woodland on a slope to a river or stream and with little or no undergrowth. Redstart also prefer this habitat but also occur in more openly wooded areas. The best time to see these species is just after their arrival in late April to mid-May, as not only is there little leaf cover but also the males are busy singing to advertise for a mate and while finding and defending a suitable nest site. The tree pipit, also a summer visitor, prefers both the woodland edge and the more open woodland. The male sings from a tree top before rising in a song flight which usually takes it parachuting down to another tree.

The nature of the terrain, with the river at the bottom of the well-wooded, steep slope, means rather frustrating views of any possible dipper or grey wagtail frequenting the many stones, unless one concentrates on a small stretch for some time.

Few waders breed in the fields close to the woodland but the calls of lapwing, curlew and at times redshank and snipe, drift across the valley from the fields further up the hillside. Look out also for skylarks and the abundant meadow pipits with their attendant cuckoos. Other birds often seen in this section include kestrel, stock dove, little owl, mistle thrush and buzzard.

2. *The path now drops into the valley and crosses the river on a new, very impressive footbridge.*

The bridge allows good views of the river and a pause to check for dipper, grey wagtail and common sandpiper is recommended. It also allows reflection on the power of water, for much of the present river bed was gouged out by a massive flood in 1967, which also washed away part of the village of Wray downstream, resulting in several fatalities. Woodland birds are similar to those described above, although there is one area with some Scots pine which is usually the best place to look for goldcrest and coal tit, both birds of coniferous woodland although they will breed in broad-leaved woodlands, especially when populations are high.

3. *The path follows the woodland edge before eventually entering Outhwaite Wood. Take the right fork, from where there is a long loop through the wood with a return to this point.*

Here the woodland is mainly sessile oak and ash, with a hazel and holly under storey, less mature than the woodland upstream although patches are suitable for pied flycatcher, redstart and wood warbler. Blackcap and garden warbler can be found where there is sufficient under storey. Nuthatches are recent colonists. Blue and great tits are common, as are long-tailed tits. The first two nest in tree holes but the long-tailed tit makes a wonderful domed nest of moss, covered with lichen and lined with several hundred feathers. It is located in two distinct positions, either in a thick bush such as a bramble patch or gorse bush, or wedged in the fork of a tree without any other protection, although the camouflage provided by the moss and lichen often makes it look as though it is just an extension of the tree branch. Tree creepers are also common, building the narrowest of nests, often squeezed into a crack or behind peeling bark. Outside the breeding season, tits, tree creepers and goldcrests form mixed bird parties to which woodpeckers and nuthatches are also attracted.

4. *The way-marked path returns through the wood but this section is closer to the river.*

This is the best section to look for woodpeckers, although the commonest, the great spotted woodpecker, can be found or heard drumming all along the valley. The green woodpecker is rather rare here. It regularly feeds on the ground searching for ants and larvae, so favours the more open sections near the river. Here the river is somewhat wider with a rocky, exposed bed, attracting oystercatchers to nest along with common sandpipers, while goosander are regularly seen. The more open areas and viewpoints allow one to scan for raptors, especially kestrel, sparrow hawk and buzzard. The latter has increased markedly in recent years, like ravens, and pairs can often be seen flying across the valley.

5. *After returning to the point where the path splits, it is necessary to return to the starting point by retracing the route through sections one and two.*

The long ridge of fells circular

Red Grouse

Start: starts and finishes at Jeffrey Hill (on Longridge
Fell), where there are parking facilities

Grid reference: SD 639402

Distance: 5km (3 miles)

Time: allow 2–3 hours

Grade: easy

General: nearest toilets and refreshment facilities at
Longridge or Chipping.

This walk commences at Jeffrey Hill car park, overlooking one of the finest viewpoints in Lancashire. The pristine and ancient landscape embraces a mosaic of lowland valley pasture and a patchwork of irregularly shaped fields, relieved only by an intricate network of roads, farms and villages and enhanced by the backcloth of the Bowland fells. On fine mornings with clear visibility, it is a joy at any time of the year to witness the spotlight of the rising sun illuminating the features of Beacon Fell, Bleasdale, Parlick, Fairsnape, Wolf Fell, Saddle Fell, Burnslack, Fair Oak Fell and the long expanse of Totridge. Perhaps it was such a morning on 17 August 1648, when Oliver Cromwell and his army passed over Thornley Fell and admired the view over the 'the Vale of Chipping', before engaging in the Battle of Preston. Hewitson in his *History of Preston* says: 'I have seen no part of the country so beautiful as this'. Many would endorse his comments while enjoying the birdwatching in a superb setting that establishes the tone of the fell and adds to the overall atmosphere. In late April, the first calling cuckoo of the year blends with the song flight of skylarks, bubbling notes of curlews and

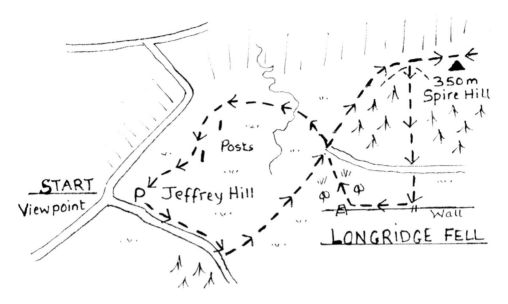

staccato bark of roe deer. For the energetic, the walk may be extended by following a range of footpaths shown on the Ordnance Survey map.

1. *From Jeffrey Hill car park, turn left up the road for about 200 metres. Look for a gate in the wall on the left, opposite the beginning of a plantation, and enter the open fell by ascending the footpath to the triangulation point of Spire Hill (350m, 1150ft, above sea level).*

2. *From the trig point take time to admire the view and then retrace your steps along the main path as far as a wooden gate on the left. Go over the stile next to it and follow the right-hand track through the plantation. Cross the stile next to a wide track and walk along the path to a stone wall, turning right immediately in front and heading towards a small, mature, conifer plantation. When you see the wall stile on the left, veer right while climbing towards the left edge of a small plantation and the wall beyond it. Follow the wall for about 30 metres and then cross the wall via a stone stile. At this point you cross the path you walked up earlier and continue straight ahead on the path across the moorland. Cross over a small stream and turn left, following the way-markers over the side of the fell until you reach the car park.*

On the rushy fell-side there are still healthy numbers of skylark, and also meadow pipit, reed bunting, linnet, the odd snipe and curlew. Buzzard sightings are increasing as this species expands its range from central Bowland. This is a good area to scan the moor for kestrels and the occasional peregrine or hen harrier, the latter using the outlying fell for hunting forays while en route to more traditional sites. Sightings of red grouse are still regular on the slopes, although they have declined in recent years. The heather moor is also the haunt of curlew, meadow pipit and stonechat, while the plantations house lesser redpoll, siskin, bullfinch, chaffinch, song thrush, great spotted woodpecker, willow warbler and magpie. Nowadays, tree pipit, whinchat, and cuckoo are less common summer visitors to Longridge Fell and unfortunately this is mirrored elsewhere in Bowland. Among the spring and summer lepidoptera are green hairstreak butterfly, red admiral, painted lady, emperor and northern oak eggar moth.

The mysterious and nocturnal long-eared owl is probably still present in very low numbers and has had mixed breeding success over the years. Rarer brief encounters with raptors have included goshawk, merlin, and at least one chance sighting of hobby. By contrast on a late winter's afternoon, the fell is quiet apart from a possible sighting of a lone kestrel or a diurnal hunting short-eared owl quartering the fell. In some winters, crossbills erupt into the plantations and their distinctive 'chip-chip' note should aid instant recognition.

Walk 8

The Crook o' Lune circular

Goosander

Start: starts and returns to Crook o' Lune Picnic Site car park

Grid reference: SD 522648

Distance: 9.5km (6 miles)

Time: allow 6–7 hours

Grade: easy to moderate

General: toilets and services at the Crook o' Lune car park.

This walk is in one of the most attractive areas of the Lune Valley. It takes in the river itself, broad- leaved and coniferous woodland and farmland, with such a wide variety of habitat that it should produce a very good variety of birds throughout the year.

1. *From Crook o' Lune car park follow the steps down to the river. Do not take the disabled trail, which does not lead to the river. Follow the well-trodden path upstream towards the Water Works bridge.*

The path here is very well used, but the walk passes the bridge into quieter countryside. Despite the number of people, this first stretch is good for kingfisher and a few small sand martin colonies. It is also a favourite feeding site for flocks of swifts, swallow and house martins, many of which breed in the Lune Valley villages. Grey wagtail and dipper like the section at the start, close to the two bridges where there is always a flock of well-fed mallard.

2. *Follow the riverside path past the Water Works bridge, noticing all the grass and other detritus caught up in the riverside bushes. This marks the extreme high water level during major floods; indeed in some areas the path has been at least five feet under, not a time to walk this route! The Lune is notorious for rising and falling quickly.*

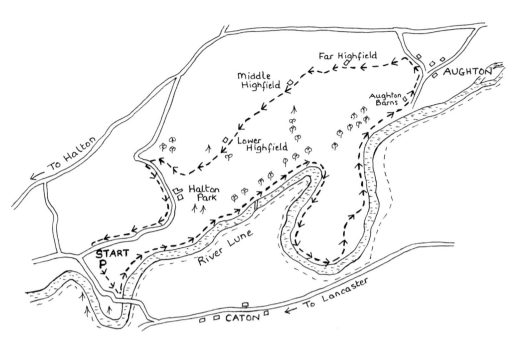

This quieter section has the first oystercatchers, goosanders, common sand-pipers and Canada geese. There is usually a larger sand martin colony, although these often move from year to year, depending on the erosion of the sandy banks. Looking away from the river the small woods here are mainly coniferous, good for both goldcrest and coal tit. Keep a sharp eye open for soaring buzzards along with kestrel and sparrow hawk, as all breed locally and are present throughout the year.

3. *The path now enters Lawson and Burton Woods, collectively know as the Aughton Woods. This is a nature reserve of the Lancashire, Manchester and North Merseyside Wildlife Trust. The path takes one close to the river, but there is the option of taking a concessionary loop path higher up the slope. The later usually produces more birds but the terrain is very steep.*

The wood is a mixed wood of mainly sessile oak, ash, elm and small-leaved lime. In spring the ground is a riot of colour with bluebells, ransoms and primroses. There are many ferns and foxgloves are common.

All three woodpeckers have been recorded, great spotted, green and the declining lesser spotted. Five species (great, blue, coal, marsh and long-tailed) of tit are regular, along with tree creeper and goldcrest. Summer visitors include pied flycatcher, redstart, chiffchaff, and at times wood warbler. Nuthatch can be easily located because of their loud distinctive calls, heard throughout the year. The loud trilling song is now very much a feature of many of our woodlands, as recently it has rapidly increased. Unlike wood-peckers and tree creepers they can run as quickly down as up the tree trunk. They use their large and powerful feet to climb and do not use the short stumpy tail like the other trunk climbing species. Its food consists mainly of insects, but as its name suggests, it also takes nuts and seeds, as it fixes firmly in cracks in the bark and hammers them until it is able to extract the kernel.

4. *Leaving the wood, the path which is part of the Lune Valley Ramble, follows the meandering of the river through low-lying grazing land.*

River birds here include more sand martins, many oystercatchers breeding on both the shingle and the grassland, common sandpiper, goosander and pied wagtail. Both yellow wagtail and ringed plover used to breed here and may still do so on occasions. However, they have both declined alarmingly in recent years, the ringed plovers because of river flooding and the yellow wagtail due to agricultural intensification, especially silage cutting. Little ringed plover also appear with other waders like greenshank and green sand-piper during passage periods. The large fields hold breeding lapwing and redshank and, outside the breeding season, flocks of lapwing, golden plover and curlew occur. From late winter to early summer oystercatchers can be found along the river. They display in small 'piping parties' an extravagance of loud calls ending in a quivering trill, in which several birds, probably neigh-bours, argue over territorial boundaries. They are also quick to defend eggs or young, chasing off crows and gulls, backed up with aggressive calling.

5. *As you approach the first house, head away from the river and take the path which becomes the road up to Aughton village. This is a steep climb with well established, high hedges and trees on either side.*

Besides the common woodland birds, both whitethroat and lesser whitethroat are summer visitors and lesser spotted woodpecker have been recorded breeding. Greenfinch and goldfinch are regular, while the village supports swallows, house martins and swifts and a thriving rookery. In winter many birds congregate around the houses, attracted by the many well-stocked feeders.

6. *Continue up the hill and after leaving the main village, turn left onto the public footpath which passes through farmland past the three farmsteads of Far, Middle and Lower Highfield. This walk through pleasant agricultural land gives spectacular views across the Lune Valley to the Bowland Fells and the York-shire fell country around the distinctive mass of Ingleborough. It passes through a small wood and eventually reaches Park Lane near Halton Park. Turn left down the hill and follow the road back to the Crook o' Lune Car park.*

The formerly high wader populations have now declined due to agricultural intensification but there are a few pockets of good wader habitat left, especially near Middle Highfield towards the Aughton to Halton Road, where lapwing, curlew and redshank still breed, with meadow pipit and skylark. In autumn and winter flocks of redwing and fieldfare strip the hedgerow berries and then search the fields for worms, often among the flocks of lapwing or black-headed and common gulls.

Golden Plover N.B.

The Tolkien birdwatching trail

Grey Wagtail

Start: start and return at Hurst Green
Grid reference: SD 685379
Distance: 11km (7 miles)
Time: allow 4 hours
Grade: easy
General: parking, toilet and refreshment facilities at Hurst Green.

This walk begins and ends at Hurst Green close to Stonyhurst College at the southern boundary of the Forest of Bowland. The village of Hurst Green and parts of the walk described are not shown on Ordnance Survey Outdoor Leisure 41. For greater detail, see OS Pathfinder No. 680 and refer to the accompanying sketch.

Stonyhurst was originally the home of the Shireburns, lords of the manor from about 1372 until 1717 when the last of the dynasty, Sir Thomas Shireburn, died. In 1791 Thomas Weld offered the house for use as a college to the Society of Jesus, which enlarged it in 1799. Stonyhurst College assumed its present appearance during the nineteenth century and includes among its pupils Sir Arthur Conan Doyle, who evidently gained literary inspiration in his new environment. A fellow pupil just happened to have the name Patrick Sherlock, while the class baddie was a certain Moriarty. The author probably caught up with them in 'the dark walk' – mentioned in the *Hound of the Baskervilles* and a wonderful dark avenue of unique ancient, gnarled yew trees. Today it is still situated in the grounds of the college laden with copious poisonous berries providing a perfect hideaway for the ever-present chaffinch and nuthatch, not to mention pupils!

Stonyhurst also has links with J. R. R. Tolkien, author of *Lord of the Rings*,

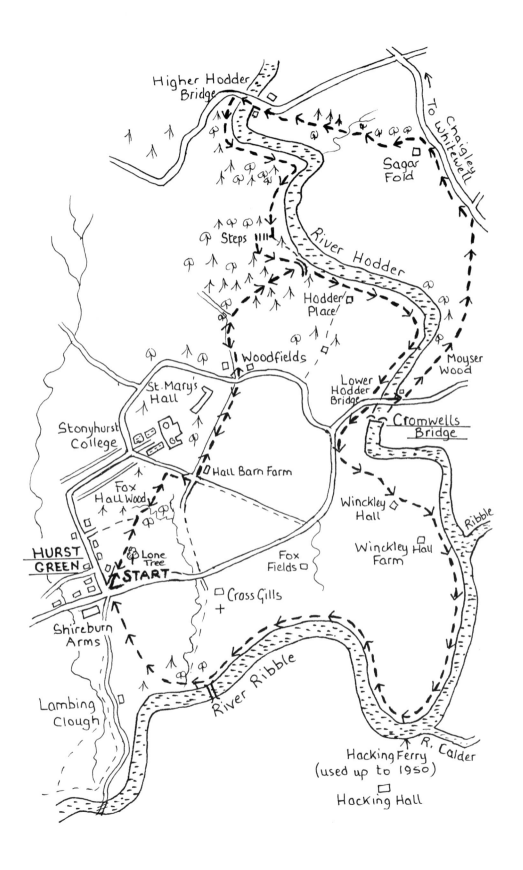

Higher Hodder
Bridge

To Whitewell

Chaigley

Sagar
Fold

River Hodder

Steps

Hodder
Place

Woodfields

Moyser
Wood

St. Mary's
Hall

Lower
Hodder
Bridge

Cromwells
Bridge

Stonyhurst
College

Hall Barn Farm

Winckley
Hall

Ribble

Fox
Hall Wood

Winckley Hall
Farm

HURST
GREEN

Lone
Tree

Fox
Fields

START

Cross Gills

Shireburn
Arms

River Ribble

Lambing
Clough

R. Calder

Hacking Ferry
(used up to 1950)

Hacking Hall

who was renowned for his love of nature and the natural landscape. Tolkien spent much of his time writing at Stonyhurst College while visiting his two sons who were pupils; indeed the Oxford professor is believed to have transposed the local landscape into his stories, with part of the area reputed to be the inspiration for Middle Earth. Peter Jackson, the producer of the enormously successful film trilogy, used New Zealand the location of the fantasy land, and there are many similarities with the Bowland landscape.

Some of the mythical features we read about in Tolkien's writings may be imagined on this walk, in what seems to be a perfect haunt for hobbits. The view from Tom Bombadil's house may have been based on that from New Lodge, where Tolkien stayed. Familiar names that occur in the film include Shire Lane in Hurst Green and the River Shirebourne, doubtless named after Sir Richard Shireburn who embarked on the building of Stonyhurst in 1590. During the 1950s a small ferry service operated across the River Ribble near to Hacking Hall known as the Hacking Ferry and was perhaps the inspiration for the Buckleberry Ferry in the *Fellowship of the Ring*. Cromwell's Bridge, built by Sir Richard Shireburn in 1561, might have inspired Tolkien to name it Brandywine Bridge on the River Brandwine. We will never really know for sure but his walks along the Hodder and Ribble, set amidst pastoral countryside with a backcloth of Pendle Hill, are believed to have influenced his writing. The Tolkien Trail follows a circular route along the rivers Hodder and Ribble, on which the River Shirebourne could well have been based. Tolkien would probably have been familiar with many of the local birds, including the sight and sound of the grey wagtail. This species and bird song are the themes of the walk that integrates a good diversity of birds to be seen in their natural hobbitat!

1. *From Warren Fold in Hurst Green, cross over a stile and follow the wall. After a gateway with kissing gate, walk diagonally right across a field, passing a large tree. Turn right on reaching the hedge and go through two kissing gates. Cross the stream and climb uphill, passing Fox Hall Wood on the left. Proceed to the gate in the right-hand corner of the field and turn right along a tarmac track to reach Hall Barn Farm. Turn left immediately before the farm buildings and emerge onto a track. Walk straight ahead to reach Woodfields, passing St Mary's College on the left. Cross over the road and turn down the lane between the houses. When the track bears left, turn right and go over a wooden style, then follow the edge of the field alongside Over Hacking Wood. Near the corner, turn left over a stile, then right to descend a stepped path.*

Early spring is a good time to do this walk. The first section traverses the environs of Hurst Green and Stonyhurst, a semi-rural habitat, usually enhanced by bird song. At Hurst Green listen for the chirpings of house sparrows, for nowadays sightings of this increasingly officially endangered species are worth recording. The copses and hedgerows hold mistle thrush, song thrush, blackbird, chaffinch, titmice, dunnock, greenfinch and robins, and lead vocalists do not need a podium here. A blackbird singing is something really special and its flute-like notes are in total contrast to the song thrush that repeats every syllable two or three times. Listen carefully for the murmurings of starlings, for the bird is an excellent mimic. Chaffinches start to 'warm up' in February with a hesitant rattle, before delivering the full trill with a terminal flourish. Nowadays that Asiatic invader of the 1960s, the collared dove, is well established and seems to call incessantly. Flocks of jackdaws are predominant in the fields and around Stonyhurst's majestic buildings.

During spring, Fox Hall Wood is clothed in a blaze of colour, ranging from the emerging fresh green foliage of sycamore to stunning copper beeches and glorious white cherry blossom. The pond provides an attractive feature, further enhanced by a range of common birds. The nuthatch has significantly increased over the last two decades and its vocal prowess usually belies its sedentary presence. Both great and blue tits have an extensive range of song, piercing the early spring with their song. Great spotted woodpeckers drum and are frequently recognised from their bouncing flight between woodland and garden. Unlike many other species, both male and female robins establish winter territories and defend them by song from late summer onwards. During cold spells most of any small birds' waking hours are taken up with feeding.

2. *Cross over the footbridge before turning right over a stone bridge and climbing the bank towards the impressive building known as Hodder Place. Descend to the river and follow a track along the river bank to the main road at Lower Hodder Bridge. Turn right along the main road to reach a footpath on the left, opposite the first road junction on the right. From here the route is fairly straightforward. Cross over the stile and follow the way-markers and Ribble Way logo across fields to reach a track leading via Winkley Hall Farm and beyond to the banks of the Hodder at its confluence with the Ribble. The footpath follows the Ribble for about two kilometres, eventually passing an aqueduct. Just west of the aqueduct strike off right through a wood and ascend the valley sides to complete the walk at Hurst Green.*

Look out for roaming bird parties in the Hodder woodlands, comprising tree creeper, nuthatch, goldcrest, coal and long-tailed tits. A disturbed roosting tawny owl may occasionally be seen, flying off on silent wings. Heron, dipper, grey and pied wagtails frequent the fast-flowing river throughout the year. Listen and look for the turquoise-blue back flash of a kingfisher flying close to the surface of the river. Common sandpipers can be seen in their characteristic posture on stones in the river and making brief stiff-winged flights, calling as they go. The attractive warbling song of the dipper is subtle to the ear and can sometimes only just be heard above the accompanying sound of the Hodder's rippling and cascading water music. In flight the call is rendered 'clink, clink', before it lands on a stone with the whole body comically dipping. If you are lucky it may perform a few party tricks by diving into the water and swimming under the water in its quest for insect larvae and small fishes.

It is a sobering thought that grey wagtails and Daubenton's bats have used the picturesque pack horse bridge at Lower Hodder since it was first constructed in 1561. It is worth a photograph while taking an opportunity to observe riverine birds and to contemplate for a moment: did Cromwell cross the bridge while en route to battle in 1648? The truth is that nobody really knows, though the reality is that a bridge seven-feet wide would probably have been a little narrow for an army of 10,000 infantry and cavalry. Cromwell and his officers probably enjoyed the luxury of not getting their feet wet, while the rain-soaked army probably had to ford the river. Some historians would consign this fanciful legend to the romantic story bin, for current debate is that the crossing was actually upstream at Higher Hodder. However, what is not disputed is that Oliver Cromwell made the decision to advance westwards along the north bank of the Ribble to cut off the Scots

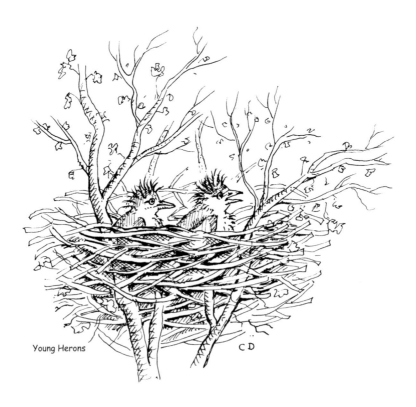

Young Herons   C D

and spent the pre-battle night sleeping on a table at Stonyhurst. Cromwell said of the building that it was 'the finest Elizabethan half house I have ever seen'.

On the approach to Winckley Hall farm around 15 pairs of herons build huge nests and rear strange-looking youngsters at the tree top heronry. The bizarre goings on at the heronry deserve observation, if only to see the adults flying in, uttering a loud 'krowrnk' and swaying on delicate-looking branches. Who knows, it may even have inspired the famous author to write about hobbits, for a young heron has an equally peculiar form and perhaps bears the closest resemblance!

Continuing along the Ribble Way, watch for a little owl in the mature trees and hedgerows that bisect fields, where there are still nesting lapwing. Black-caps and chiffchaffs are two spring migrants that haunt the wooded areas close to the Hodder and Ribble. Close to the confluence of the Calder there are numerous sand martins flying over the river from colonies in the river banks. Depending on the time of year, bird highlights along this section of the Ribble Way include black tern, greenshank and green sandpiper, as well as kingfisher, dipper, grey wagtail, oystercatcher, curlew, whimbrel, common sandpiper, redshank, goosander and goldeneye.

Walk 9A

Returning via Higher Hodder bridge

Distance: 11km (7 miles)
Time: allow 4 hours
Grade: easy

From Lower Hodder Bridge there is an option to take an alternative circular route.

1. *Cross Lower Hodder Bridge and walk a short distance along the main road towards Clitheroe. Turn left at the first public footpath sign on the left after Hodder Bank Cottages and skirt the edge of Moyser Wood. Cross over two stiles and across a field, to rejoin the main road at its junction with New Lane. Walk along the main road towards Chaigley and turn left at the next public footpath sign after Sagar Fold. Cross, over farmland, streams and copses to Higher Hodder Bridge. Turn left and cross Higher Hodder Bridge, then take the public footpath immediately thereafter, to return along the banks of the Hodder. You will pass through woodlands, followed by an open area with a field on one side and the river bank on the other, before ascending through the last stretch of Hodder woodland. Take care crossing the steep woodland bank and proceed via an ancient stone cross to the stone bridge. Turn right and climb innumerable steps to eventually reach Hurst Green via the outward route.*

Look and listen for the flash of colour and raucous calls of a group of jays, and that other less commendable crow, the magpie. Roe deer have now expanded into the lowland river valleys of Bowland and should be looked for at the edges of woodland or venturing forth into more open areas. Throughout both walks the sparrow hawk may be seen almost anywhere and as we rejoin the Hodder there is also a chance of seeing an unwelcome mammalian predator, the mink. It is unfortunate that this alien is now well established on the Ribble and the Hodder and may readily be seen, while otter sightings are rare. Walking along the banks of the Hodder, look out for goosander, especially in winter, and the usual flocks of mallard. The alders should be scanned for any feeding siskins, lesser redpolls and flocks of long-tailed tits. The ubiquitous grey wagtail needs only the smallest of streams to forage and adds sparkle to the walk. It is usual to see them standing on a stone in mid-stream or flying ahead, uttering 'chissick', a sound reminiscent of the pied wagtail but more metallic. Leaving the woods, pause and listen to the cacophony of spring bird song. It may help to ease the burden of climbing so many steps.

Walk 10

On hearing the first cuckoo in spring

The Dunsop Bridge via Burholme circular

Cuckoo.

Start: starts and finishes at Dunsop Bridge
Grid reference: SD 661501
Distance: 6.5km (4 miles)
Time: allow 4 hours
Grade: easy to moderate
General: parking, toilet and refreshment facilities at
Dunsop Bridge.

This walk begins and ends at Dunsop Bridge, which in 1992 was declared by the Ordnance Survey to be the village nearest to the exact centre of the British Isles. However, the precise location is above the Brennand Valley at SD 6377056550. The birds likely to be seen reflect the diversity of habitat through which we pass, including scenic stretches of the Hodder valley. We pass close to Burholme, the site of a hamlet of medieval origin. A feature of the walk is the gothic Knowlmere Manor, built in the late Victorian era and once the home of the Peel family, descendants of Sir Robert Peel, the founder of the police force. On this walk you can wander along over isolated moorland and the valley of the Hodder without seeing a soul. This is perhaps one of the joys of Bowland, even at the height of the season, for few places have that distinction nowadays.

1. *From the car park, walk east along the road to Thorneyholme by forking right at the first junction. Cross the bridge and at the end of the railings turn right through the gate and walk the footpath following the River Hodder, to the single seventeenth-century farmstead at Burholme.*

Flocks of swift, swallow and house martin, along with charms of goldfinches

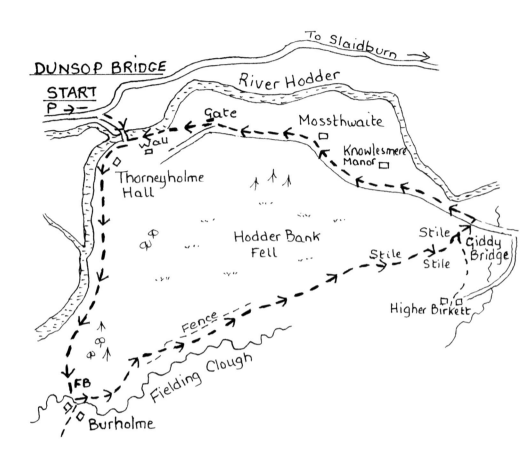

and the less attractive jackdaw, are invariably present around the village of Dunsop Bridge. The wooded area at Thorneyholme harbours the usual summer visitors, including the occasional pied flycatcher. The river provides opportunities to see resident dipper, grey and pied wagtail, kingfisher, moorhen, Canada goose, mallard and goosander. During spring and summer, common sandpiper, redshank, curlew and oystercatcher are seen regularly. The scattered trees and copses on the hillside of Mossthwaite Fell and Fielding Clough hold cuckoo, redstart, tree creeper, chaffinch, mistle thrush, green and great spotted woodpecker. Around Burholme Farm and on the nearby flooded field, look for goldfinch, starling, kestrel, common gull, lapwing curlew, mallard and teal.

2. *Approaching the farm at Burholme, turn left before the bridge over Fielding Clough and cross over a stile. Follow the yellow way-markers to cross a second stile over a wire fence. Climb uphill with the fence on the left and*

Fielding Clough on the right. Walk onto the open moorland of Hodder Bank Fell and pass through a gate, keeping close to a barn on the right. After the barn, cross three stiles while descending to the Hodder valley. Where the foot-path divides (third stile), go straight ahead onto a concessionary path. Turn left towards Knowlemere Manor and follow the yellow way-markers towards Mossthwaite and Dunsop Bridge.

In and around the alders in Fielding Clough leading onto the open moor expect to see pheasant, stonechat, meadow pipit and tree pipit. Kestrel, buzzard, peregrine and short-eared owl are all quite likely over the heather moors to the right, while on Hodder Bank itself odd pairs of Canada geese have now taken residence. Reaching the Hodder valley look in the direction of Newton and you will see a knoll of trees. The area between Knoll Wood and Newton has been a favoured haunt of the red kite during recent winters and one day it might establish itself in this prime habitat.

3. *Beyond Mossthwaite, cross a stile on the right and head diagonally right across the field to a fence/stile. Follow the yellow way-markers along the edge of a field and river bank to go through a gate at Thorneyholme. Turn right over the bridge and return to the starting point at Dunsop Bridge.*

In the vicinity of Knowlemere Manor the woods hold redstart, jay, great spotted woodpecker, mistle thrush and nuthatch. Bird parties flitting through the trees comprise titmice, goldcrest, tree creeper and wren. Finches are represented by chaffinch, greenfinch, goldfinch, bullfinch, linnet, siskin, lesser redpoll and in some winters, brambling. Flowing though the estate the Hodder has goosander, dipper, pied and grey wagtail, and grey heron stand around motionless as they quietly fish the river before flying off on broad wings. As you pass the farmsteads, trees and pasture on the final section of the walk past Mossthwaite, look for pied wagtails, reed bunting, redstart, spotted flycatcher, stock dove, curlew and little owl. Nowadays it is not too unusual to see flocks of up to 12 buzzards soaring over the Hodder and Dunsop valleys in the vicinity of Dunsop Bridge.

Walk 11

The Littledale trail

Woodcock.   CD.

Start: starts and ends in the small parking area East
of Crossgill
Grid reference: SD 624560
Distance: 6.5km (4 miles)
Time: allow 4–5 hours
Grade: moderate
General: toilets at Crook o' Lune car park:
other services in Caton.

This well-used track gives a pleasant circular walk, including the upper sections of the valley of Artle Beck as it passes through Littledale. The mixed woodlands, fast-flowing stream, open rushy fell and sheep-grazed fields of Caton Moor support a good range of species.

1. *There is limited parking at the start of the footpath, so alternatively park in the Little Crag Access Area car park and walk to the start. The path passes first through coniferous woodland, then there is a short section with conifers to the left and broad-leaved trees to the right.*

This section is an excellent area to compare the bird life of coniferous and broad-leaved woodland. In spring the amount of song coming from the broad-leaved valley woods from thrushes, tits, finches and warblers (blackcap, garden warbler, chiffchaff and willow warbler) contrasts with the almost total silence from the dense, dark coniferous spruce. However, two species do commonly nest within the conifers: the coal tit and the gold-crest, our smallest bird, whose high-pitched song is usually the first indication of its presence. The delightful acrobatic siskin is a recent colonist of conifers, and again, its distinctive call betrays its presence. Many of the woodlands have an under storey of rhododendrons which, being an alien

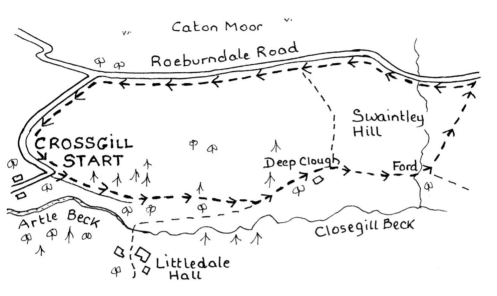

species, hold little attraction for birds, although blackcaps and garden warblers use them.

2. *The well-marked track leads along the valley side, starting at the small, partly ruined chapel, now used as a cow shed.*

This rather unexpected building has an interesting history, built by John Dobson in the 1840s, a vicar who fell out with the established church. Reverend Dobson was obviously a man of means for he purchased the Liddledale Estate, erected his own chapel and ministered to his tenants. His son John died at the age of 19 and is buried in the railed-off tomb at the back of the chapel, which is also a memorial to his father.

A fine selection of woodland and woodland-edge birds occurs here, including mistle thrush, jay, tree creeper and tree pipit. Where there is suffi- cient under storey, both blackcap and garden warbler will be found. The open fields are too steep to hold breeding waders but in spring the pervasive calls of the curlew drift in from the fells. This section gives good views across the valley to the moorland shoulder of Clougha. The imposing Littledale Hall is now rather dominated by the agro-industrial buildings around it, many of which hold laying hens, whose eggs are used in the production of flu vaccine. Pied wagtail and spotted flycatcher occur around the hall.

3. *The well-used path continues up the valley, positioned part way up the hillside.*

The typically upland woodland hosts redstart, pied flycatcher and occasional wood warblers. Meadow pipits breed in the open areas and are the main attraction for breeding cuckoos. The path passes some way from the stream so clear views are limited but it is worth scanning the larger sections of visible water and rock for dippers, grey wagtail and common sandpiper. The all-round visibility of the open areas gives good views of buzzards and kestrels, both of which breed locally, while ravens often fly over, identified quickly by their unique deep croak. A visit at dusk or dawn on a fine evening from late March to June should produce a 'roding' woodcock or two. This woodland wader spends all day crouching quietly in the woods, its wonderful cryptic markings rendering it invisible unless disturbed, when it rises swiftly and dodges through the trees. At dusk and in the early morning, the male takes to the wing to patrol his territory and attract a female. He gives a deep, constantly repeated harsh croak followed by a shrill 'chizzic' note. At times males meet, which results in a bout of chasing and quickened activity. With the gathering darkness tawny owls practise their wide range of calls, while the sudden bark of a startled roe deer adds to the mystery of the evening.

4. *The footpath starts in open woodland then passes Deep Clough Farm and enters upland farmland, passing Swaintley Hill before joining the Roeburndale Road.*

The woodland birds are very similar to those in the previous sections but in the open farmland waders like lapwing, curlew, redshank and snipe become more evident. Look out for stock doves, house sparrows, starlings and swallows around the farm buildings. Much has been written recently about the decline of house sparrows and starlings in suburbia but they are still common birds around many of the farmsteads in Bowland, where agricultural intensification has been slow. Pied wagtails are also a typical farm bird, often breeding in holes in the farm buildings. Outside the breeding season, grey wagtails often frequent the manure piles, feasting on the many flies.

5. *Turn left onto the Roeburndale road, then continue until the next left which takes you back to the start point. The wind farm on Caton Moor rather dominates the views to the north.*

The rushy fields hold many lapwing, but curlew are the most abundant and obvious waders, with fewer snipe and redshank. The many stone walls are used as perching and nesting sites by pied wagtail, wheatear and little owl, often seen throughout the day. Skylarks are still common here, although well outnumbered by meadow pipits. From late spring, large flocks of starlings, lapwings and rooks frequent the sheep-grazed fields, joined by transitory flocks of meadow pipits and smaller flocks of skylarks after the breeding season. This abundance of prey, along with a high small mammal population on the open moor, attracts several predators. Peregrines, kestrel, buzzard and sparrow hawk are the most regular, with merlin, hen harrier and short-eared owl less frequent.

Walk 12

To the fells from historic Whitewell

Stonechat   C.D.

Start: starts and ends at Whitewell
Grid reference: SD 658468
Distance: 7.5 km (4.5 miles)
Time: allow 5 hours
Grade: moderate
General: parking, toilet, and refreshment facilities at
Whitewell, Chipping and Dunsop Bridge.

This circular walk embraces lonely hill country, lowland pasture and riverine stretches along the Hodder, offering a diversity of habitat for a range of Bowland's characteristic birds. The walk over Birkett Fell to Crimpton is rough in places and as the path is not well defined it is advisable to carry a compass. *The walk is linked with Walks 10 and 21 and reference should be made to these walks for a description of the birds to be seen.*

Within the environs of the Hodder at Whitewell, there is a good chance of seeing sparrow hawk, lapwing, curlew, oystercatcher, redshank, common sandpiper, kingfisher, dipper, pied and grey wagtail, nuthatch, tree creeper, song thrush, collared dove, green woodpecker, great spotted woodpecker, wren, robin, titmice, siskin and greenfinch. Summer sees swift, swallow, sand martin, spotted flycatcher, pied flycatcher, redstart, chiffchaff, blackcap, garden warbler, willow warbler and occasional migrant wood warblers passing through the gorge. Coal tits are commonly encountered but the marsh tit, seen occasionally near the Inn at Whitewell, is in definite decline. In winter expect to see big flocks of redwing and fieldfare and mixed flocks of chaffinch, greenfinch, bullfinch and brambling.

The forecourt of the inn was once the local market for the district. The

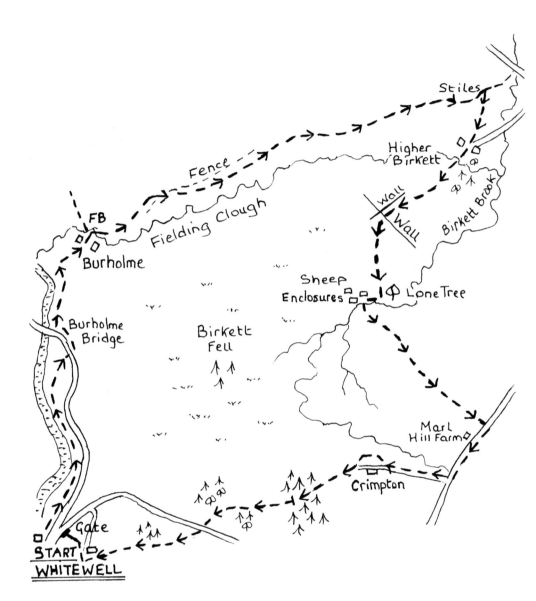

hotel was built on the site occupied by the former fourteenth-century manor house where the Keeper of the 'Royal Forest of Bowland', Walter Urswyck, once resided. The earliest parts of the Inn at Whitewell are said to date back to the 1300s and Walter would have resided in what would then have been a small manor house. He also established a chapel at Whitewell next to inn at the beginning of the fifteenth century, although the present chapel dates back to 1818.

Officers of the 'Chase of Bolland' had responsibility for the red and fallow deer within the curtilage of Radholme Deer Park that formerly embraced Whitewell (see Walk 21). Since those medieval times Radholme Laund is now predominantly dairy pasture, though archaeological evidence of the deer park may still be discerned. Nowadays, however, roe deer and the introduced Sika deer have long replaced the indigenous red and fallow deer of the ancient parks.

At twilight the last vestige of daylight is usually taken up by a solitary vocal robin with its melancholy, rusty, monotonous song cycle, and a 'roding wood-cock', silhouetted just above the tree line, carrying out its territorial flight across the wooded ravine. The smaller mammalian contingent comprises the pygmy and common shrew, bank vole and the ubiquitous wood mouse. Noctule bats flying over the riverine woodlands are joined by Daubentons (water) bats skimming the surface of the water, and pippistrelle and long-eared bats. A single pippistrelle will enjoy the local cuisine of up to 3,000 midges in one night.

We may choose to start or finish the day off in fine style over a drink at the Inn at Whitewell, where culinary tastes are well catered for and where we can discuss the merits of the walk while focussing on the birds. If during autumn and winter the species list is a little thin on the ground then at least the historic landscape, with the Roman road taking its arduous course through the hills at Cowark north to the Trough, will have provided more than a measure of compensation. Perfect sobriety will ensure that you do not see any cave dwellers or fairies either, for there is evidence that cave dwellers lived in this area around 1000 BC. And within recent times Bronze Age archaeological finds have been made within the 'Fairy Caves' above the Whitewell gorge and indeed in the river itself. A Bronze Age stone used for the grinding of grain was found in the Hodder in 1984 by Mr Bowman of the Inn at Whitewell and has been dubbed 'The Whitewell Stone'.

1. *From Whitewell, it is recommended to take the Bowland bus to Burholme Bridge to avoid walking along the main road. At the two-arched bridge, do not cross but take the farm track to the right of the bridge. At Burholme farm cross the stile and follow the course of Walk 10 by walking right and over a second stile and traversing the open moorland of Hodder Bank Fell, before descending to the Hodder valley. Where the footpath divides, leave the course of Walk 10 by turning right and walking the short distance to cross the next stile on the right. Cross a field and pass through the farmyard at Higher Birkett Farm. Follow the track to ford a stream, passing a wood on the left before the track peters out in a field. Keep right to a wall and follow the wall to a ladder stile in the top right-hand corner of the field. Climb over and walk diagonally left, descending the side of Birkett Fell to a stream – head for the*

single tree. Go right to a walled sheep enclosure. At this point cross the stream and climb the bank opposite, along an indistinct path that veers right over a small clough. Follow the way-markers to the unclassified road and turn right, passing Marl Hill Farm on the right. At the bottom of the hill go right to Crimp-tons, then follow the directions for Walk 21 as far as Whitewell to return to the starting point.

The ghostly sight of the largely resident barn owl or white owl is still affectionately regarded by farmers, country people and naturalists alike, but unfortunately sightings in Bowland are now rare. A chance encounter may include its upright stance on a fence post caught in the headlights of a car or hunting by daylight, flapping along the edges of open fields and dykes. Since Spencer (1973) suggested that the barn owl was nowhere very rare in Lancashire there have been major decreases in many areas, including Bowland. Nowadays it is a rare breeding resident in some peripheral areas of the Forest of Bowland, while commoner in the Pilling and Cockerham area. However, it is virtually extinct in several former haunts including Gisburn Forest, where in the late 1960s up to four pairs nested in the old barns and farmsteads. Immigration of dark-breasted continental birds sometimes occurs and they should be looked for along with the indigenous species in winter on the coastal mosses.

Barn Owl

The reasons for both national and local declines include a high incidence of road mortality, loss of nest sites and habitat through urbanisation and barn conversions, and changes in agricultural practice. However, the erection of nest boxes in West Lancashire's barns by Messrs R. Danson and T. Myerscough has partially redressed the decline in these areas. It is testament to their conservation initiative, the goodwill of the farming community and minimal disturbance at nest sites, that barn owls may still be encountered in these limited areas of Lancashire. The adoption of similar schemes in Bowland might now be considered to facilitate their re-introduction.

Walk numbers: 16, 21, 28, 29.

The blackcap is a common summer visitor, passage migrant in coastal areas and increasingly a winter visitor. Throughout Bowland blackcaps are commonly found in similar habitats to its close relative the garden warbler, usually in deciduous or mixed woodland and suitable hedgerows and large gardens with an abundance of ground cover for nest sites.

Small numbers have wintered in the area since the 1960s feeding on berries and fat balls at feeding stations in gardens. Essentially the blackcap is a summer visitor, arriving at the end of March and peaking throughout April. On arrival male blackcaps can be seen fairly well before the foliage begins to emerge either in low bushes or in the tops of trees. Distinguishing the song from that of the garden warbler can cause difficulty to many birders. However the latter tends to be longer and more rhythmic, unlike the blackcap which is sweet but a little jerky and more strident.

Black Cap

Walk numbers: 2, 6, 8, 9, 9A, 11, 13, 14, 16, 18–22, 23, 23A, 24, 25, 26, 27.

Bullfinch

Throughout Bowland bullfinches are quite widely distributed in both coniferous and deciduous woodlands, and are also prominent along hedgerows and suitable gardens where their secretive presence is often belied by their distinctive piping call. Overall this local prosperity tends to buck the trend of national and regional decline since the 1970s. In winter and spring bullfinches visit orchards and gardens where they consume both buds and berries. Decreases are said to coincide with desecration of habitat, including the tidying up and loss of hedgerows. Consistent with this hypothesis is that in Bowland, where hedgerows are not flailed in autumn, bullfinch populations remain relatively high.

Walk numbers: 2, 6, 7, 8, 9, 9A, 10, 11, 13, 14, 16, 18–23, 23A, 24, 25, 26, 27.

The buzzard is a large, broad-winged raptor with a rounded broad tail, which over the last 20–30 years has expanded into Bowland, where it is now established as a resident breeding bird. The Bowland population seems to be going from strength to strength, mirroring the rest of Britain. Buzzards were virtually extinct as a breeding species by the end of the nineteenth century and progressive elimination by sporting and farming interests continued into the early twentieth century. The species was given full legal protection in 1953 but the population crashed over the next decade with the widespread use of organochlorine pesticides and the outbreak of myxmatosis in rabbits, its favoured prey. Following the withdrawal of these chemicals and a resurgence of rabbits, buzzard numbers increased during the 1980s. South-east Bowland was colonised by 1997 so the area now supports a well-established population. Since 1994 pairs have also occupied the western slopes of Bowland and the species is now commonly seen in the Lune valley. Buzzards prefer to breed in deciduous or mixed woodland from low to fairly high altitude and may often be seen in early spring soaring and displaying over the nest site. Population maxima are attained in the late summer and autumn, when the young disperse to other inland and coastal locations. Wintering does occur in the hill districts, especially where rabbit concentrations occur, although severe weather displaces many birds to the moorland fringe and lowlands. It is also likely that winter records involve immigrant individuals from elsewhere in Britain and beyond. We can now look forward to seeing 'the tourist's eagle' and hearing its characteristic mewing on most of the walks described.

Walk numbers: All walks excluding 9, 15 and 30.

Buzzard

Chaffinch

The familiar chaffinch is without doubt one of the commonest and most colourful birds of Bowland and is typically found wherever there are trees and shrubs in woodlands, hedgerows, gardens and picnic sites, often uttering its anxious 'spink' call. It is a familiar bird in the Trough of Bowland and has become particularly tame due to being fed in the vicinity of picnic sites, and may even be found in copses extending onto higher open moorland.

The chaffinch is a resident, passage migrant and winter visitor throughout the area of Bowland and the coastal plain. In winter chaffinches typically feed with the less common brambling on the crop of beech mast or on the ground in large agricultural fields. When in flight white rumps should be looked for to distinguish the chaffinch from the brambling and closer focus will reveal the contrasting plumage between the two species.

The chaffinch is likely to be found on all of the walks.

The diminutive coal tit is easily identified by a white patch running up the nape and bisecting the black cap, while the black bib contrasts with prominent white cheeks.

Harsh winters seriously impact on coal tit populations but recent trends for mild ones have seen the species prosper and it is now an abundant breeding resident throughout Bowland's afforested areas. Post-breeding dispersal can lead to large numbers irrupting out of the forests during the autumn with numbers sometimes being seen on the coast. In Bowland conifer trees are the preferred habitat and up to ten or twenty birds is not unusual at feeding stations in Gisburn Forest, with smaller numbers visiting garden bird tables. Coal tits are also found in deciduous woodland and churchyards and ornamental gardens such as the dark walk at Stonyhurst College.

Coal Tit

Walk numbers: 1–3, 6, 7–14, 16, 18–24, 25, 26, 27.

Common Sandpiper

Characteristically the common sandpiper searches for insects and perches on boulders in rivers, dipping its body and bobbing its tail up and down.

The common sandpiper is both a common summer visitor and passage migrant to Bowland's rivers and their tributaries and reservoirs, with occasional instances of over wintering away from the breeding sites. The first birds of spring usually arrive at breeding haunts by the first week of April, with the breeding cycle extending over a period of about ten weeks. When the young fly the sandpipers vacate the breeding grounds and head for the coast. On passage up to fifteen birds have been seen at Stocks Reservoir in July and they also occur in late summer and autumn at Pilling Lane Ends, in the creek at Conder Green and on the Lune mudflats.

Nest sites are often close to public amenity areas and consequently are becoming increasingly vulnerable. Indiscriminate tramping of tall herb-rich vegetation that provides cover for nesting should therefore be avoided especially when the adult birds are in close proximity and displaying obvious signs of alarm.

Walk numbers: 1–4, 6, 8–13, 16, 18–23, 24, 25, 26–29.

The instantly recognisable call of the male cuckoo demands attention and is warmly regarded as one of the harbingers of spring. Cuckoos have sadly declined in many parts of Britain but the fells and fell edge of Bowland remain strongholds. A long-tailed, sharp-winged, slate-grey bird, barred on the breast, it can be easily confused with the sparrowhawk. Small birds will persistently chase and mob both a flying or perched cuckoo, probably a reaction to its predator-like looks and famous habit of nest parasitism. In Bowland, the abundant meadow pipits are invariably used as fosterers, one reason for the relative abundance of cuckoos on our moorland.

Though the male calls both in flight and when perched, it is often difficult to locate. When calling from a perch he has a very characteristic pose – he bows forward, lowering the head and drooping the wings while fanning the elevated tail. The throat is swelled as he delivers the familiar call, whereas the female's call is a distinctive bubbling note, quite unlike the male's. Large, hairy caterpillars are its favoured prey. The adults leave for the African winter areas in July and August, while juveniles linger to late August and September.

Walk numbers: 1–3, 6, 7, 10, 12, 14–18, 20–27.

Cuckoo

Curlew

The evocative, wild, liquid bubbling call of the curlew in spring and early summer is one of Bowland's most familiar sounds. Indeed from late February to July, it is *the* characteristic bird of the moors and farmland. This unmistakable wader, with its six-inch long, de-curved bill and bulky brown body, is unlikely to be missed on any Bowland walk during the breeding season. Soon after arrival in early spring, the male indulges in an aerial dance, rising and falling on stiffened wings with a loud trilling song and this nuptial flight continues throughout incubation. The curlew has a wide repertoire, including the call from which it takes its name, while other alarm calls warn of danger, which become more evident as the nesting season progresses when the pair's sentinel detects danger and warns its incubating mate. The calling becomes even more frantic after hatching, as both parents seek to warn of, and if possible drive off, a possible predator. As the young fledge, and move away, the moorland becomes strangely quiet. Recent RSPB surveys found a breeding population of 2,850 pairs, making it the commonest wader in Bowland, which has the highest breeding population in the United Kingdom.

After breeding, most birds move to coastal wintering grounds but some remain in the river valleys where they can be found in flocks or small groups on regularly favoured fields, which are deserted only during spells of hard frost.

All walks.

The dipper is the typical resident of fast-flowing streams and rivers, so well adapted to this ever-moving environment. This short tailed, rather rotund bird is equally at home bobbing on rocks or diving into the fast-flowing water. Once under the water it 'swims' with its wings as it searches the stream bottom for the larvae of aquatic insects, a line of rising bubbles tracing its course underwater. Out on the rocks surrounded by swirling water it continually bobs or curtsies and this sudden dipping action gives the bird its name.

Resident on all the fast-flowing streams and rivers within Bowland, it is strongly territorial, staking its claim by uttering its rather scratchy, hurried wren-like song as it scurries along the stream edge. Its territorial boundaries are quickly clear for the bird will move down a stream then, when it reaches the edge of its neighbour's domain, it will double back into the safety of its own territory. Usually it leaves the upland territories only when the streams are frozen during severe cold spells.

The nest is always close to water; indeed some are built under the water on the rocks behind a small waterfall. Other regular sites include holes in the rock or in the masonry of a bridge. The dome-shaped nest has an entrance hole low down at the front and is built of moss, dead grass and leaves. An early nester, the first clutch is often laid in mid-March. On a suitable fast-flowing stream the breeding density can be as high as one pair per 1.5 km of stream, partly dependent on food availability, and the highest density occurs on streams flowing over limestone. The Lancashire breeding bird atlas suggests a Bowland population of perhaps 75 to 100 pairs.

Walk numbers: 1–4, 6, 8–13, 16, 17, 20, 22–27.

Dipper

Dotterel

The dotterel is a rare summer visitor, mainly restricted to the Cairngorms and Grampian mountains and usually at an altitude above 3,000 feet. The 'trips' of dotterel (the collective noun for flocks) we see near to the triangulation pillar on Pendle Hill or Ward's Stone and occasionally elsewhere on Bowland's highest summits are spring passage migrants feeding on insects, to sustain them during their long northward migration from Africa. The best time to see this prized species of plover is during the last two weeks of April or first half of May. Timings and location are crucial to see the bird in its Lancashire upland splendour but great care should be taken to avoid unnecessary encroachment and disturbance by making them fly. Dotterel are quite fearless and the best maxim is let them come to you!

The dotterel has striking yellow legs, a white band across the upper breast and a broad white supercilium, ashy brown upper-parts contrasting with a chestnut patch below shading into black on the belly. In flight it shows a dark rump and tail and faint wing bar. When it comes to being sexually dimorphic, the female has the edge as she is brighter in appearance and more dominant than the male. The male undertakes all incubation duties and tending of the young.

Pendle Hill has become well known nationally for its annual sightings of dotterel. In recent years trips have rarely exceeded fourteen, contrasting with the early 1980s when flocks of up to 43 birds were seen. The return autumn passage on Pendle is rare, though an unprecedented trip of three adults and nine juveniles was on Pendle on 25 August 1996.

Walk numbers: 3, 5, 15, 17.

As a member of the thrush family the fieldfare is quite unmistakable, with its black spotted underparts, grey head and rump, reddish brown back, yellow bill, and distinctive chak-chak-chak call. It is a Scandinavian winter visitor and passage migrant to a range of habitats from Bowland's open wooded country and fields to moorland edge at Stocks Reservoir.

Flocks of fieldfare are observed from early October to April feeding with another Scandinavian thrush and close relative, the redwing. Widespread reports of mobile flocks of fieldfare over 1,000 strong occur during October and November flying between berry-laden trees and hedgerows or in fields taking grubs and worms. Numbers tend to dwindle during December when dispersal occurs over a wider area.

During late March and early April fieldfares may be seen acquiring their brighter summer plumage. Pre-departure flocks of around 500 tend to be the norm, with odd individuals lingering into May.

At the right time of year fieldfares can be seen on all of the walks, including flying over the highest fells.

Fieldfare

Goldfinch

Since the 1970s the goldfinch has sustained healthy populations in Bowland as a common breeding resident and passage migrant. This beautiful small finch is quite unmistakable with its black wings and gold bands, and black, red and white head. 'Charms' of goldfinches working the thistle heads and teasel are a lovely sight. Goldfinches may commonly be found in Bowland's diverse habitats of open cultivated country, hedges, woodland edge and gardens. They are often encountered in close proximity to man, markedly so, when a garden feeding station is well stocked with its favourite delicacy, niger seeds or sunflower hearts.

Substantial numbers winter in France and Iberia while others remain in the area and are helped to survive by the recent tendency for milder winters. The breeding season extends from May to August and thereafter flocking takes place with birds feeding locally and exemplified by 300 noted throughout Bowland on 28 August 2002.

Walk numbers: 1–4, 7–14, 16–29.

The goldcrest is quite at home in Bowland's conifer forests, breeding in the mixed woodlands of spruce, larch and pine. However, with the firecrest it shares the distinction of being our smallest British bird (about 3½ inches) and may be difficult to find. Also, the possibility of it being the much rarer but similar firecrest should not be overlooked. However, the yellow crown is different from that of the red crown of the latter, that also exhibits a distinct white eye stripe bordered by black lines. As always with small passerines the song is crucial in location and identification.

It is a common breeding bird, spring and autumn passage migrant and winter visitor. The nest is worthy of mention for it is a unique, rounded hammock of moss and cobwebs, lined with feathers, and suspended by three or four handles near the end of a conifer bough. Large influxes of goldcrest reach Britain from the continent during September and augment local populations. Goldcrests may be found on all the Gisburn Forest walks and elsewhere in habitats comprising woodlands, hedgerows, churchyards, gardens and in Autumn on the coast. In autumn single birds associate typically with bird parties of tits and tree creepers as they wander about, often in broad-leafed woodlands.

Walk numbers: 1–3, 5–14, 16, 18–29.

Goldcrest

In full breeding plumage of black under-parts and black spangled, golden-yellow upper-parts, the golden plover is a joy to behold. Favoured areas usually feature the shorter heather created by the regular practice of rotational heather burning, so the relatively small breeding population of around 50–60 pairs often moves as the heather height increases. They are also found on blanket bog with cotton grass and the bare peat areas of the higher fells. Breeding pairs are patchily distributed throughout the fells, but nowhere can they be described as common. During breeding, the adults regularly commute to adjacent pasture for feeding, whilst the chicks are often taken to the more grassy areas after hatching. The first sign that a pair is present is usually the often repeated liquid whistling alarm note, but even so the pair can be difficult to locate among the heather. On hearing the call the best plan is to scan the shorter vegetated areas, watching the skyline for birds in flight.

The breeding birds move to the fells in early March, regularly using upland pasture fields as a stopping off point, especially during unseasonable weather. Breeding pairs move out in July and flocks can be found in regularly favoured fields both in the Lune valley and low-lying fields near the coast until early spring. They regularly associate with lapwings but on the wing the species usually separate, with the fast-flying golden plover out-flying the slowly flapping lapwings.

Walk numbers: 1–5, 8, 11, 13, 15, 17, 26–30.

Goosander are now well established as breeding residents on Bowland's rivers and are regular winter visitors to rivers and larger expanses of water such as Stocks Reservoir. Breeding is a relatively new phenomenon, however, and was first recorded in Lancashire in the early 1970s.

Wintering flocks of over thirty or so are not unusual on the upper reaches of the Ribble and on the Lune, where much valuable research has been undertaken in recent years. These parties remain together until they break up into pairs around February. Nesting usually takes place in a hollow tree

or under boulders in a bank and in nest boxes, often up to 5 metres from the ground. Remarkably the young ducklings leave the nest 24 hours after hatching and the large broods of around ten ducklings tumble to the ground and are led to water by the female. Goosander swim low in the water and dive for the fish which form most of their diet.

Walk numbers: 1, 2, 8–10, 12, 16, 18–29.

Goshawk

In 1838 a Victorian ornithologist wrote of the goshawk: 'Very rare, though shot or caught occasionally in the Forest of Bowland.' Subjected to continuous persecution, goshawks had ceased to breed in Lancashire and most of Britain by the end of the nineteenth century. In Bowland, records date from 30 June 1957, when one was seen at Chipping. The first breeding pair was recorded in the mid-1960s and since then a small number of nesting pairs have successively occupied territories in areas of commercial forest.

The goshawk provides an exciting spectacle in April, as it soars and flies with slow wing beats and engages in a wonderful display flight, rising and falling in vertical swoops. The male goshawk may easily be confused with the closely related female sparrowhawk. It is, however, about 25% larger and structural characteristics, including the goshawk's protruding head and broader deeper chest, are significantly different. Soaring, the goshawk has a long, broad barred tail and rounded wings, conspicuous, white under-tail coverts and a broad, white supercilium.

Rapacious hunters, goshawks regularly prey on a diversity of creatures, from wood pigeons and crows to passerines and small mammals. Outside the breeding season they are rarely encountered, suggesting dispersal to coastal regions or hunting over a much wider inland area. Unfortunately, on grouse moors and in the pheasant rearing areas of Bowland, there is still likely to be a level of antipathy towards birds of prey, with egg collectors still posing a considerable threat. The future of the goshawk in the Forest of Bowland is, therefore, at best precarious.

Walk numbers: 1, 3, 7, 20, 24, 27. (Drawing by Christine Dodding)

The grasshopper warbler is a summer visitor and uncommon breeding bird that arrives back at a few breeding sites in young plantations of Gisburn forest usually during the last week of April. The preferred habitat consists of dense ground cover interspersed with very young conifers from which the males utter their territorial song.

When not delivering its bizarre reeling song that genuinely sounds like a grasshopper or other insect, 'groppers' are notoriously difficult to locate as they creep about the long grass and ground cover like a mouse. It is only when they emerge onto a branch or tussock to sing that one has a reasonable chance of locating the bird. Breeding information is speculative and is usually based on the numbers of reeling males present over a given period. Up to three have been located near Stocks Reservoir in recent years.

Walk numbers: 20, 26.

Grasshopper Warbler

Great Spotted Woodpecker

The great spotted is the commonest of the three woodpeckers that occur in Bowland. Their numbers have increased considerably over the last twenty years and it is now a common resident throughout Bowland's woodlands, copses, open parkland and farmland – wherever there are trees. In recent years it has taken to visiting garden bird tables, especially those with nuts and fats on the menu.

The undulating flight and repeated sharp 'pic pic' call is diagnostic. In spring both sexes will drum on a chosen tree or even a telegraph pole with a series of very rapid blows with their extra strong bill. Display involves chases in the air and round the wood, all accompanied by excited calling.

Walk numbers: 1–3, 6–14, 16, 18–27.

The well-known 'yaffle' call of this colourful woodpecker is often the first clue to its presence, for despite its colourful plumage it is quite a difficult bird to track down. It is well worth searching for though, as it is one of our most colourful birds with its distinctive mainly green plumage, bright yellow rump and crimson crown. Although it is found in wooded areas it spends a lot of time on the ground, where it searches out the abundant ants of rough pasture and woodland edge. It is commonest in the Lune and Ribble valleys.

Walk numbers: 2, 6, 8, 11, 13, 19, 22, 26.

Green Woodpecker

The grey heron is the only species of heron regularly occurring in Bowland. It is unmistakable as it stands patiently in the shallows or on a post in characteristic, hunched posture. It flies with the neck tucked in.

Grey Heron

Throughout Bowland grey herons may be seen on slow-moving rivers and streams, ponds, lakes, reservoirs, sheltered tidal waters and increasingly even on garden ponds. Fishing herons often wade in shallow water with their eyes focused along the bill waiting for an opportunity to stab a prize catch with tremendous accuracy and speed. Once caught, larger fish are taken to the bank and repeatedly stabbed. Eels present the greatest challenge, as they wind themselves round the heron's bill and are only swallowed after a lot of shaking and stabbing, the whole process at times taking up to five minutes. Although fish make up the majority of the diet, herons will also take young water birds and adult birds up to the size of a water rail. Well-used local names for the bird include crane, jammi-crane and frank, the later describing the bird's call, which is regularly given as it takes off.

Breeding populations have remained stable at a number of heronries within the Forest of Bowland, the most important of which is that at Claughton on Brock. During 2003 the Claughton heronry was estimated at 50 pairs, indicating a reversal of recent downward trends at this heronry which dates back to at least 1850.

Potentially all the walks provide an opportunity to see a grey heron, either on the ground or in flight.

Fast-flowing streams and rivers are the haunts of this water-loving bird. The grey wagtail runs nimbly along the stream margins, flicking from stone to stone, then quickly darts upward to snatch a fly. It searches the shallows and the rock edges for flies and crustaceans. It is a slimmer, graceful and more colourful bird than the well-known pied wagtail, although both species constantly wag their tails in characteristic style.

The nest is usually in a crevice in a rock, bank or wall, often in bridges and occasionally under small waterfalls, often with an overhang to provide shelter. Two broods are reared, then, after

fledging, the young birds disperse along the streams and rivers, many moving away from the upland streams at the onset of autumn before returning to nest in early spring. It is a common bird throughout Bowland in suitable breeding habitats, its presence often revealed by a distinctive, metallic sounding 'tzit-tzit' call.

All walks except 7, 14 and 15.

Grey Wagtail

Hen Harrier

The pulse quickens at the sight of a male hen harrier performing its magnificent 'sky dance'. During April the sudden vision of a dazzling, pearly grey bird amidst Bowland's mosaic of wilderness, rising and falling in an azure sky into a frenzy of display, is stunning. The 'sky-dancer' could be riding an imaginary switchback while rolling on his back at the top of an ascent. A female suddenly appears from nowhere and prey is exchanged, talon to talon. As the male completes the food pass, the ritual is complete. It is indeed a privilege to watch. This rare breeding species is widely regarded as the classic bird of the Forest of Bowland.

Male and female hen harriers are remarkably different in both size and plumage. The female (ringtail) is brown with a larger white rump, contrasting with the handsome grey appearance of the smaller male. Harriers distinctively fly with wings held in a shallow 'v' while quartering and gliding. The private estates where nesting takes place, mainly heather moorland, represent the most important breeding population in England. Wing tagging has demonstrated that Scottish birds disperse to Bowland: for example, a tagged female of Scottish origin nested in Bowland for several consecutive years from 1994. During autumn, Bowland's immature birds disperse widely to the coastal plains and are seen on the Ribble estuary and at Martin Mere. Conversely there are now regular winter sightings of hen harriers in the Trough of Bowland, Stocks Reservoir and Champion Moor, even during severe winters, so no regular pattern emerges.

Despite full legal protection since 1953, a catalogue of destruction at human hands has contributed to its present tenuous status. Historically the area was important in the Victorian era, when the first confirmed breeding took place in Upper Wyresdale in June 1876. Then harriers were shot by fowlers at Martin Mere and on inland mosses, so by the turn of the century the species was almost extinct in Britain. Oakes (1953) described their status as 'formerly resident now a passage bird in small numbers', while reports from the private estates suggest harriers were rarely seen in Bowland in the 1950s/1960s. The first confirmed instance of breeding in Lancashire since Victorian times was in 1969 when a nest with young was found. In 1971 nesting was attempted on Longridge Fell but it was not until 1974 that Bowland started to be fully re-colonised and two nests produced a total of five young. In 1996 six nests were successful and nineteen young were reared, approximately two-thirds of the young reared in the whole of England that year.

Following political, media and other interventions, the species has enjoyed mixed fortunes. In 2002 six pairs nested on the private estates, producing nine young, some of which were radio tagged to trace migratory movement and monitor their progress. However, by 2004, the English population was confined to Bowland, where around eight pairs successfully raised about twenty-eight young. The results of three years of monitoring by English Nature's Hen Harrier Recovery Project has confirmed that illegal persecution is the main reason the population is so low in England.

Walk numbers: 1, 3, 4, 7, 10, 12, 15, 16, 21, 24–30.

Jay

This colourful member of the crow family is usually shy and rather secretive, its rather raucous call usually betraying its presence, especially during the breeding season. Exclusively a woodland species, it feeds on acorns in winter and its habit of caching them when abundant is believed to be a major factor in the propagation of oak trees. The jay is mainly restricted to the more extensive, broad-leafed woodlands, especially along the Lune and Ribble valleys.

Walk numbers: 1, 2, 6, 8, 9, 11–14, 17, 19, 20, 22, 23, 24, 26.

The word 'kestrel' is derived from 'coystril', a medieval term meaning 'cowardly knave or being inept at its art'. The kestrel or wind-hover is still a relatively common resident throughout the Forest of Bowland. Hunting, they normally take short flights, hovering over suitable terrain before suddenly pouncing on a vole or mouse. In this respect they are unlike the resident sparrowhawks and merlins which pursue birds with frightening agility. Oakes (1952) described their Lancashire status as 'a common resident everywhere, breeding up to 1300 feet on the hills and becoming more urban'. He also quoted records of kestrels capturing house sparrows and starlings.

Bowland's old quarries, hollow trees and abandoned farmsteads give kestrels a wide selection of nest sites in both lowland and upland areas. Dispersal and passage take the birds to the coast between mid-August and October. Ringing evidence shows some birds are sedentary while others migrate to continental shores.

Kestrel

There is now evidence of reduced numbers of kestrels but nothing to indicate a serious decline. In the past this species has adapted well to change, as even non-birdwatching drivers on the motorways and urban dwellers may have perceived. Local prosperity for kestrels depends on a healthy Bowland environment, including rough vegetation and margins with long grass at the edges of agricultural land, ideal habitat for small mammals, which sustains local populations.

All walks.

Kingfisher

The kingfisher is one of our most strikingly colourful and well-known birds. Occasionally, they alight on a convenient post or overhanging branch and show off their classic features of superb cobalt blue upper-parts, brick red under-parts, long bill, short tail and brilliant red legs. Fishing for minnows and sticklebacks then commences by plunge diving into the water. The call is a distinctive single 'tee' and exemplifies the importance of calls in locating and identifying birds.

A series of mild winters has contributed to the prosperity of the kingfisher and in Bowland its status is that of a widely distributed breeding resident throughout suitable habitats. Principal haunts include the main rivers and their tributaries and occasionally lakes and reservoirs. Specific habitat requirements equate with slow moving, clear rivers or streams, with banks for nesting away from swift-flowing upland streams.

Kingfishers excavate nest holes leading to a nesting chamber about one metre long in soil or sandy banks. Laying usually begins in April with incubation by both sexes. The accumulation of bones of fish fed to the young adorn the nest chamber and at times are visible at the entrance. The young fledge after about three weeks.

Harsh winters have a devastating effect on local populations. However, with most pairs double brooded and rearing six or seven per brood, the population soon recovers. Disturbance along river banks has obvious implications for breeding kingfishers. In recent years alien and voracious mink have posed a threat as unwelcome predators that impact on riparian breeding bird populations. Therefore effective control of their numbers to maintain the sensitive ecological balance of our river banks can be justified.

Walk numbers: 2, 8, 9, 10, 12, 16, 22, 25–30.

Lapwing

This well-known wader is a common breeding bird, widely distributed throughout Bowland. With declines observed elsewhere due to agricultural intensification, Bowland can rightly be described as the English stronghold of this attractive species. With its bizarre tall crest, rounded wings and distinctive call, it is easily identified. At a distance it looks just like another apparently black and white bird, but at close quarters it is transformed – the back is glossy green and the rich chestnut patches above and below the tail are stunning.

Arriving on the breeding grounds during the first mild spell of late winter, the males establish their territories with erratic aerial dances, accompanied by excited bouts of calling. The bird rises suddenly, dashing upward then hurtling earthward, swinging from side to side and beating the air with a loud humming sound before dropping lightly. He then starts to attract the female by scraping a hollow in frenzied haste by bending forward with his breast to the ground and sporting his rich chestnut tail patches to entrance the female. The male forms the nesting scrape, which is usually lined by the female with small pieces of dead grass. Both sexes share the incubation and care of the young, which leave the nest scrape shortly after hatching and are well able to find food when only a few hours old. The young are regularly brooded by the adults until well feathered.

Numbers have declined in recent years on the in-bye land due to regular silage cutting but they are most abundant on the rough grazing fields and the lower stretches of moorland. Recent census work by the RSPB suggests a population of at least 2,500 pairs.

All walks

These two closely related species, lesser black-backed and herring gulls, are dealt with together as they have a large mixed breeding colony on Tarnbrook and Mallowdale Fells. Recent counts suggest a nesting population of about 20,000 pairs, of which about 20% are herring gulls, and with them are about 10 pairs of greater black-backed gulls. This mixed colony is the largest inland gull colony in Britain, an impressive sight especially when large numbers become airborne during a disturbance, such as the appearance of a passing hen harrier. In spring and summer numbers can be seen any where in Bowland, hawking merging insects over the fells, to gathering soil invertebrates in bye fields. There is also a continual passage of birds to and from the Lancashire coast where they collect much of their food.

Numbers have fluctuated in recent years, partly due to culling to protect water catchment interests; in the early 1980s it was believed that there were up to 30,000 pairs. The lesser black-backed gull used to be almost exclusively a summer visitor but in recent years increasing numbers have stayed the winter, depending on easy pickings on landfill sites. In contrast, herring gulls tend only to disperse to the coast for the winter, though both return in numbers during the first mild spell of late winter.

All walks

Lesser Black-backed Gull

Little Owl

This delightful owl is an introduced species which has increased and become well established in open and sparsely wooded areas, and is commonest in the Lune and Ribble valleys. It often hunts by day perching on stone walls or buildings from where it can locate its main prey which are earthworms and large insects, although some will specialise in taking young birds.

Walk numbers: 2, 4, 8, 13, 17, 28–30.

Long-eared Owl

The long-eared owl is one of the rarest of Bowland's breeding birds. This highly secretive, nocturnal bird mainly frequents mature conifer plantations and the combination of these factors makes it one of the most difficult birds to locate, and so it is probably often overlooked. The call of the male, a long drawn-out quivering hoot, is very distinctive, but is usually only used well after dark in the very early spring at the start of the breeding season. During the day it sits bolt upright on a branch close to the trunk of a tree and so is very difficult to detect especially in a dense conifer plantation. When well grown the hungry young are often quite vocal and the call is referred to among bird watchers as 'the un-oiled hinge or creaky gate call'. The so-called ear tufts are not ears at all, but distinctive tufts of feathers.

Recent sightings have been from walks 17 and 26.

Meadow Pipit

The meadow pipit is Bowland's commonest breeding bird, abundant on even the highest moors, where on a warm spring day dozens will flutter up from the heather, the air full of their trilling song, delivered as they rise and float down on outstretched wings. They are quite confident but become concerned if the nest, which is well concealed in grass or heather, is approached. As the season progresses there is less song but the birds are conspicuous when they begin feeding their young. The meadow pipit is the favoured host species of the cuckoo and the favoured prey of the merlin.

Maximum numbers occur after the breeding season when large flocks congregate on the lower moors or adjoining fields. Birds from further north join the local breeders, and throughout September and much of October large flocks can be seen migrating either towards the coast or heading south. Few can be found in the area in winter for ringing has shown that many of our birds winter in France and Iberia.

All walks

This recent colonist now breeds in small numbers, mainly at Stocks Reservoir. In recent years the breeding population has been only 2–3 pairs in the whole of Bowland. Mainly a fish eater it resorts to the coast in winter where it can be seen in numbers, and it only rarely occurs inland at this season.

Walk numbers: 22, 26, 28–30.

Merganser

Merlin

Towards the end of the nineteenth century the merlin bred in small numbers on extensive areas of moorland. During the 1950/60s there was a significant decline due to the use of agricultural pesticides. Once these were banned numbers slowly increased and by 1981 a minimum of nine nests was confirmed. By 1998 a healthy breeding population raised 28 young on United Utilities land. The nest is usually, though not exclusively, deep in heather, often on a steep slope, thus affording a sitting bird a good lookout. On the outlying fells breeding is only spasmodic and away from favoured heather moorland merlins rely more on bracken-covered slopes for nesting, or occupy the old nests of crows in trees. The meadow pipit is the main prey and on occasions merlins will opportunistically pursue small birds flushed by hunting hen harriers, displaying remarkable aerial agility.

During July and August virtually all merlins move to lower latitudes to winter on Lancashire's coastal fringes and marshes. Ringing recoveries have shown juvenile birds to leave their natal quarters very early and have been recovered from sites as far afield as the Mersey by mid-July. In 1989 a photographer noticed a pair of ringed merlins at a Bowland nest site. The female had been ringed in Shetland as a nestling in 1987, while the male was of local Bowland stock. The pair nested together on the same Bowland fell for at least three consecutive years.

Some persecution has been recorded recently, but fortunately appears to be limited. Increased afforestation schemes, as well as disturbance and illegal activity by egg collectors and others, continue to pose a threat to Britain's smallest raptor. Extensive rank heather moorland at the heart of Bowland is crucial for the survival of this endangered falcon, for the population is of national importance. It is vital that the breeding sites in areas like Bowland are safeguarded from widespread habitat change and human interference.

Walk numbers: 1, 3, 4, 7, 15, 17, 19, 24–30.

A common, well-distributed resident of woodland, gardens and well-timbered farmland, it is absent as a breeding bird from only the higher treeless moorland. The name is derived from its habit of feeding on mistletoe berries, but its local name of storm cock is very fitting, for it will happily perch

Mistle Thrush

high and sing its rolling, forceful song in the teeth of a gale or other inclement weather. At times it will sing in flight as it goes from one song post to another. The mistle thrush is larger, greyer and more distinctly spotted than the song thrush. It is a more robust bird with a loud rather grating call. From late summer on it feeds on berries starting with the mountain ash along the moorland edge. Parties of birds will gather to reap this harvest. Later hawthorn, yew and exotic garden berries are taken. At times a bird will attempt to defend a tree against all comers. When the berries are exhausted it searches fields and gardens for worms and molluscs but in late winter takes the ripening Ivy berries.

Can be seen on almost all the walks.

Peregrine Falcon

This superb raptor, the largest of our breeding falcons, is resident throughout Bowland. The peregrine's wings are long and pointed and overall the bird looks much heavier than a kestrel with a shorter tail. At close quarters a broad, black, moustachial stripe is visible. It is famous for its hunting method of circling high over its intended prey then swooping at great speed and striking in flight. Peregrines were uncommon in Bowland during the first half of the twentieth century and the 1950/1960s saw a catastrophic decline and breeding failure, again through the use of lethal, organochlorine pesticides in agriculture. They suffered high adult mortality and low breeding success as the chemicals resulted in thin egg-shells and failure to hatch young. In 1962 only about 400 nests were traced throughout the UK, very few producing any young. A ban on the use of certain pesticides produced a dramatic reversal of what was a desperate situation.

Nesting sometimes involves only moderate success: of seven nests located on United Utilities land in 2002, four nests failed due to disturbance and poor weather, whilst five young were raised from the other three. Peregrines pair for life, utilising the same nest site year after year. The British population is now one of the largest in Europe, with Bowland proving instrumental in its recovery. The conservation success story of this particular species is such that it now shares many of our villages and towns with local communities. Expansion from Bowland's wildest areas has led to nesting pairs in such diverse sites as a church in Blackpool town centre and a Victorian mill chimney in Darwen.

Walk numbers: 1, 3, 4, 5, 6, 10, 12, 14, 15, 16, 18–21, 23–30.

This semi-domestic bird is well represented in Bowland, as the warning notices 'Take care Pheasants on the Road' well indicate. It has long been part of the British avifauna, having been introduced possibly as early as the thirteenth century for its sporting prowess. Very large numbers are still hand-reared and released each year to satisfy the sportsmen and they rarely stray far from where they are released.

The pheasant is a ground bird, preferring to run on its strong legs rather than fly if danger threatens. When it does take to the wing it rises with a marked whirr of wings and rockets over the tops of the trees before quickly landing again, but only rarely will it indulge in sustained flight. It usually roosts in trees to escape ground predators.

The males are polygamous, although whether this is the natural state or is part of the gamekeepers' management strategy is difficult to determine, for 'cocks only shoots' late in the shooting season are a regular part of game management. Certainly the female incubates and rears the young on her own.

This familiar species can be seen on almost all the walks.

Pheasant

Pied Flycatcher

This attractive summer visitor arrives back from its African wintering areas in late April or early May. The male usually arrives a few days before the female, its conspicuous black and white plumage and lively, oft-repeated song making it easy to locate. The male first selects a nest hole, either a natural one such as an old woodpecker hole or a nestbox. Sometimes males dispute a hole with bouts of chasing, posturing and occasionally fighting. Once in possession, the male sets about attracting the much duller plumaged female by singing and sporting himself, often from a dead bough. He moves with quick, rather tit-like movements and a constant flicking of the tail. Once paired, no time is lost in building the attractive nest from oak leaves and honeysuckle and lining it with grass, wool and hair. When incubating, and especially feeding young during May and June, pairs are easy to locate and watch, but once the young fledge the families quickly resort to the treetops and become almost impossible to find.

This species, which prefers mature woodland, especially sessile oak, seems especially attracted to valley woods close to running water. Its distribution especially in the side valleys of the Lune, Ribble, Hodder and Brock has been greatly helped by the provision of nest boxes. Indeed the wide-scale provision of nest boxes has certainly increased both the numbers and distribution of the pied wagtail. In the northern valleys there were no breeding records before 1966, but with the provision of nest boxes by members of the Lancaster and District Bird Watching Society, the population increased rapidly, showing that the lack of suitable nesting holes had restricted the population. Recent survey work for the Lancashire breeding bird atlas suggests a population of about 75 pairs in Bowland.

Walk numbers: 3, 4, 6, 8, 10–12, 16–19, 21–27.

The Pied Wagtail is by far the commonest and most widely distributed of our three wagtail species. Although essentially it is very much a water bird – be it river, lake, pond or small puddle – it utilises other habitats widely, some of them with very little water. These include upland fields, with their miles of stone walls providing very suitable nesting sites, and the grazing animals with their associated flies providing an excellent source of food. Manure heaps and farmyards are favourites with their host of insects and plenty of nest sites in the farm buildings.

The black and white plumage and long tail make this an easy bird to identify. Local names such as willie or water wagtail and dish washer reveal its liking for water and its close association with man.

Can be seen on almost all the walks.

Pied Wagtail

Red Grouse

Hunting has been associated with the Forest of Bowland for centuries. The days of the great grouse shoots date back to the beginning of the twentieth century when record bags were obtained from Mallowdale Fell above Abbeystead. On 12 August 1915 it was boasted that 2,929 birds were brought down in six drives over eight guns. By the end of October of the same year a total of 15,176 red grouse had been shot on these moors. Despite the endeavours of landowners and gamekeepers to maintain the bags of yesteryear and produce a harvestable population for the 'Glorious Twelfth', numbers shot have fallen dramatically. In modern times habitat degredation especially over-grazing and afforestation have contributed to the decline. Also grouse suffer from infestation of an internal nematode parasite and the young have a high mortality rate during prolonged wet spells.

The fells close to the Trough of Bowland and Abbeystead are at the centre of distribution, with fewer on outlying fells such as Longridge Fell and Pendle Hill. The species relies mainly on heather, bilberry and crowberry but can also be found near blanket bogs with cotton grass. They are resident on the fells, with pairs often formed in winter and remaining on territory. After alighting or before flying off with rapid wing beats and glides, this prize game bird usually utters a not inappropriate 'kok, kok, kok, goback, goback, goback goback' call. Grouse are easily identified and may often be seen at close quarters, standing proudly with a distinctive and rather comical red wattle.

Red grouse prefer long heather for nesting and young shoots, insects, spiders and seeds for food. Maintaining the right ecological balance is accomplished by rotational heather burning, which produces different ages of heather. The whole management plan of a grouse moor is aimed at preserving the shooter's quarry, the main reason why Bowland's moors have not been given over to sterile commercial forestry.

Walk numbers: 1, 3, 4, 5, 7, 15, 17, 19, 24, 25. (*Drawing by Christine Dodding*)

The red-legged partridge is now a regular sight in many parts of Bowland. It was first introduced into southern England from Europe during the eighteenth century. Since the 1960s there have been numerous attempts by gamekeepers to release this traditionally sedentary southern species into arable lowland and some upland areas of northern England. Introductions including chukar/red-legged partridge hybrids are to maintain shooting interests and to compensate for the demise of the grey partridge. It is to be hoped that any hybrid confusion has now been alleviated with the withdrawal of the licence for hybrid introductions in 1992.

Red-legged partridges can be found in most habitats, excluding the heather moorland. Unfortunately numbers now exceed those of the indigenous grey partridge, which, although never common in the Bowland area, no longer enjoys this status elsewhere. It may be distinguished from the latter species by a contrasting marked head, grey back and bolder markings on the flanks. It is also quite vocal and its call of 'kcho kcho kcho' resembles a steam train, slowly ascending a gradient but ultimately running out of steam. Small-scale introductions have often been ephemeral and they, too, have run out of steam.

Walk numbers: 3, 10, 12, 17, 19, 21–28.

Red-legged Partridge

Redpoll

The redpoll is predominantly a bird of young and developing woodland. In Bowland it breeds widely in conifer plantations, usually 10–25 years after planting, but declines rapidly as the trees mature, so populations can be quite transitory. Where conditions are suitable it can be quite common, often nesting in a rather loose colony.

This active little finch can quickly be distinguished from the rather similar twite and linnet by its black chin. The male has a striking crimson forehead and breast, the latter lacking in the female. In flight it is very active and rather erratic, regularly 'dancing' while delivering its rather simple trilling song.

Outside the breeding season it forms flocks with siskins and goldfinches and resorts to stands of birch and riverside alders. It is a very acrobatic feeder, often hanging upside down from the swaying branches to reach the seeds. At such times they can be quite approachable, especially when they drop to the ground in search of fallen seeds.

Walk numbers: 1, 2, 3, 4, 7, 9, 9A, 10, 11, 12, 13, 14, 16, 17, 18, 19, 20, 21, 22, 23, 23A, 24, 25, 26, 27, 29.

The redstart is well distributed in suitable habitat throughout Bowland. A particularly attractive summer visitor, it prefers open woodland and areas of scattered trees along the moorland edge, especially wooded cloughs where it nests in holes in trees, stone walls or masonry. Nest boxes are used but not as regularly as by tits and pied flycatchers. At times it is a difficult bird to find, but following the male's rather feeble song may produce quick glimpses of it high up in a tree, particularly in late April or early May. The rich chestnut tail and rump is usually seen first, while the male has an attractive white forehead, black face and rich chestnut breast. The female is much duller but both sport the distinctive red tail, constantly in motion, especially when fly catching, for the redstart is an excellent flycatcher with much of its food consisting of aerial insects.

Redstart

Birds become more widespread in late summer with young birds regularly seen along roadside hedges, again with the chestnut rump showing clearly. Recent surveys suggest a population of perhaps 200 pairs – quite significant in national terms.

Walk numbers: 1, 3, 4, 7–13, 16–27.

Reed Bunting

In Bowland the reed bunting is very much a bird of wet, rush-dominated flushes and the reed-fringed edges of reservoirs, pool or dykes, but nowhere can it be described as common. Its local name of reed sparrow describes the habitat well.

The breeding areas are deserted from late summer onwards, but early birds return during the first mild spell in February or March. Most winter on lowland farmland and along the coast. Numbers have declined in recent years and this is thought to be mainly due to the shortage of suitable wintering areas, partly attributable to the move away from arable farming and the widespread use of herbicides which reduces considerably the amount of weed seed available to the birds. Recent ringing returns suggest that birds are moving further south in winter, with recoveries from the south coast, possibly also a reaction to the decline of winter food noted above.

Walk numbers: 1, 2, 3, 4, 7, 9, 10, 11, 12, 13, 14, 15, 16, 17, 18, 21, 22, 23, 23A, 24, 25, 26, 27, 28, 29.

The first sign of the ring ouzel is usually the loud, harsh alarm rattle, followed by the wild song, both in keeping with its habitat, the lonely gullies and rock outcrops within heather moorland. It can be difficult to locate, partly because of its rather shy, nervous behaviour, but also because at times its song seems to echo around the hillsides. When flushed, the flight is strong and rapid as it dashes down the gullies, skimming the ground to dodge out of sight wherever possible. However at other times it can be quite approachable, especially when gathering food for the young or in areas where it is used to human presence. A summer visitor, it arrives in the hills in early April, staying until early September.

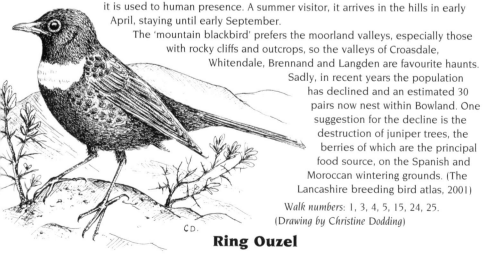

The 'mountain blackbird' prefers the moorland valleys, especially those with rocky cliffs and outcrops, so the valleys of Croasdale, Whitendale, Brennand and Langden are favourite haunts. Sadly, in recent years the population has declined and an estimated 30 pairs now nest within Bowland. One suggestion for the decline is the destruction of juniper trees, the berries of which are the principal food source, on the Spanish and Moroccan wintering grounds. (The Lancashire breeding bird atlas, 2001)

Walk numbers: 1, 3, 4, 5, 15, 24, 25.
(Drawing by Christine Dodding)

Ring Ouzel

Short-eared Owl

Short-eared owls have probably enhanced the landscape of the ancient Forest of Bowland for centuries. Mitchell (1885) mentions a nest robbed of six eggs on Pendle Hill in 1877 and comments on the former lowland heather mosslands as a breeding stronghold. Oakes (1953) recorded nesting on Ward's Stone and on several of the outlying fells, including Parlick and Fairsnape Fell.

Today it is a scarce upland breeding bird on both open moorland and in areas of young plantations. Bowland hosts a significant breeding population – according to the Lancashire breeding birds atlas (2001) 'numbers fluctuate between five and 25 pairs ... and fluctuations are related to cyclical vole populations'. They feed mainly on small mammals, and nesting productivity may extend to two broods. During recent mild winters this diurnal species has sustained good numbers around Stocks Reservoir and on Champion Moor. They are nomadic and there is evidence of autumn dispersal to coastal marshes by some local birds and winter immigration from Scandinavia by others. When the vole population crashes in northern Europe, numbers probably reach Bowland, supplementing local populations and exploiting prey densities. They can be seen quartering over open ground in characteristic style, similar to a hen harrier, and at Champion Moor both species may be observed from the public highway. During the autumn of 2002 up to eight were present here until the end of the year. Short-eared owls will often perch on a wall or fence post, exhibiting big, yellow, staring eyes. On take-off dark marks on the underside of the relatively long wings are conspicuous. When displaying, the male is likely to engage in both vocal utterances and the remarkable wing clapping – a fine spectacle amidst the wild Bowland landscape.

Walk numbers: 1, 3, 4, 7, 10, 11, 12, 14–21, 24–30.

The shoveler is a rather scarce non-breeding visitor to inland reservoirs in Bowland. Most records are from Stocks Reservoir, where it occurs annually in small numbers. It has stayed throughout the breeding season on the Lune and is a winter visitor to the coastal marshes. Many of these birds probably originate from Leighton Moss further north in Lancashire, which is the region's principal breeding and wintering area.

On the water the bird is often remarkably active, swimming in short rushes or apparently moving round in circles. This is all part of its feeding strategy, for the large bill is an effective sieve: water mixed with mud and weeds is rapidly drawn through the bill, anything edible being sifted out before the water is expelled at the base of the bill. This is quite a noisy process, although the observer has to be close by to hear it.

Walk numbers: 2, 26, 28.

Shoveler

The siskin is a very recent colonist of Bowland having first been recorded breeding in the late 1970s. It is very much a bird of mature conifer plantations including the widely planted Sitka Spruce. In recent years it has increased and now nests widely but still in small numbers in the extensive forests around Stock Reservoir, on Beacon Fell and in Lunesdale. With the area of maturing conifers increasing there is every chance that the bird will continue to increase in numbers and range.

Siskin

This acrobatic little finch is also a regular winter visitor and passage migrant. For much of the winter flocks frequent stands of birch and riverside alders. They will regularly visit the same group of trees for several weeks, when the siskin often hangs upside down to pick out the alder and birch seeds.

In late winter natural food appears to be running out and the siskin moves in numbers to gardens where it will happily take peanuts and a wide range of seeds. Ringing has shown that there is a marked northerly movement at this time of year of birds which have wintered as far south as northern France and Belgium. Some of these birds are drawn from the Scottish breeding population and a Garstang bird ringed in February was found two months later in Russia.

Walk numbers: 1, 7, 8, 9, 9A, 10, 11, 12, 14, 16, 18, 19, 20, 21, 22, 23, 23A, 24, 25, 26, 27.

A skylark in song is unmistakable as it rises high on quivering wings until it is a vocal speck against a blue sky. Its wonderful song, delivered continuously and with true vigour, is remarkable; the energy needed to stay aloft while in full voice must be large, and yet some birds seem to sing in spring for many hours in a day. When at a height the song ceases and the bird drops abruptly until a short distance from the ground where it skims forward before alighting. Skylarks are at home in open country and they shun well-wooded areas.

Skylark

Despite a catastrophic national decline the skylark is still quite common in many parts of Bowland. It has mainly gone from the hay meadows and in bye grazing land, a victim of silage cutting and heavy grazing pressures. However it is still common on the less heavily grazed grass moorland where there is a good mixture of grass and heather at lower altitudes that is absent from higher heather moorland areas.

Walk numbers: 3, 4, 5, 7, 11, 12, 13, 14, 15, 16, 17, 18, 19, 21, 28–30.

Snipe

This bird is now mainly found on wet, grassy moorland and blanket bog, with a few pairs in the wetter bye-fields. Land drainage, silage making and more intensive grazing have driven it away from most of the meadows and from the bye land it used to occupy. Even so, Bowland is still an important area for this threatened wader, a recent survey suggesting a population of around 200 pairs. It is very much a target species for the Bowland Wader Project where landowners and farmers are being encouraged and advised by the RSPB and other interested parties to reverse some of the recent detrimental practices and make farming more wader friendly. Already the results are most encouraging.

One of the most evocative features of the snipe's spring territorial behaviour are the two territorial calls that it uses. The first is the 'chipper chipper' call, a vocal note usually delivered while perched on a fence post or wall but also sometimes given in flight. The 'drumming' or 'bleating' of the male is a superb sound, best heard on a still morning or evening. The male rises with rapid wing beats, which is quickly followed by a sharp descent when the sound is produced by the stiff outer tail feathers standing out at about 45° and vibrating in the rush of air as the bird shoots down. It is appropriately know locally as the 'heather bleater'.

Walk numbers: 2, 3, 4, 5, 7, 10, 11, 12, 13, 14, 15, 16, 17, 18, 21, 24, 25, 26, 29.

Sparrow Hawk

For breeding the sparrowhawk is confined to woodland, with a definite preference for conifer plantations, but it hunts widely in woodland and farmland and at times even out onto the open moorland. In Bowland it is much restricted as a breeding bird to the lower wooded areas and river valleys.

The sparrowhawk is a low-level hunter. It flies low, fast and silently along hedgerows or threads its way through trees in the hope of surprising some unsuspecting bird. Its main prey are small birds up to the size of blackbirds or starlings or occasionally wood pigeons. Starlings are often taken as they mass to roost in reeds or conifer plantations; such a mass of potential prey can often attract several birds. In this situation a different hunting technique is also employed with the sparrowhawk bird flying high and attempting to get above the wheeling starlings and then diving through the massed flocks. Several attempts are usually required before a meal is secured.

Walk numbers: 1, 1A, 2, 3, 6, 7, 8, 9, 9A, 10, 11, 12, 13, 14, 16, 18, 19, 20, 21, 22, 23, 23A, 24, 25, 26, 27.

The spotted flycatcher is one of the last of the summer visitors to arrive, usually not until early May. It is very much a broad-leaved woodland and garden species, only thinly spread in Bowland and is nowhere common. It seems to prefer the larger river valleys, especially the Lune and Ribble, and is regular in the larger country gardens in these areas. Recent surveys suggest that it has declined considerably in recent years in many areas.

Its sombre grey-brown plumage with few if any spots makes it inconspicuous, but its habit of perching conspicuously and its fly-catching activities quickly catch the eye. It has a distinctive 'zit' call and a short low song.

Many birds catch flying insects but none so expertly as the spotted flycatcher. It perches on a post or dead branch overlooking an open area earning itself the name 'post bird' locally. When an insect is spotted it sallies out following each turn of its prey before making a smart final catch, often with an audible click of the bill. Butterflies, moths and beetles are taken, but its main prey are the abundant two-winged diptera flies..

Walk numbers: 1, 2, 6, 8, 9, 9A, 10, 11, 12, 13, 16, 18, 19–21, 22, 23, 24, 25.

Spotted Flycatcher

An increase in the stock dove population was noted by Mitchell in 1885, with expansion continuing into the twentieth century. It enjoyed mixed fortunes during the mid-twentieth century, with contractions associated with the species' preference for a mainly agricultural environment. Throughout the North West, the amount of seasonal food and nesting sites available have been reduced by modern farming practices, including uprooting trees and hedgerows, demolition or renovation of suitable old farm buildings and in particular the use of chemicals on the land.

In Bowland the elegant and gentle stock dove is still a fairly well distributed breeding resident. To some extent this may be seen as a legacy of the prosperity of the area's nineteenth-century stone trade and quarrying. Spencer (1952) pointed out that 'the extensive evacuation of hill farms in the district in the interests of reservoir construction has resulted in ready-made nesting sites.' As stock doves are mainly sedentary, seasonal movements are restricted to flocks moving from areas of higher altitude to more suitable winter feeding. Breeding occurs in the river valleys and along the moorland fringe, with sites including quarries, cliffs, holes in trees and masonry, as well as derelict farm buildings. The species is likely to be encountered on most of the walks either as singles or in small flocks.

Walk numbers: 1, 3, 4, 5, 6–14, 16–18, 20–28, 30. (*Drawing by Christine Dodding*)

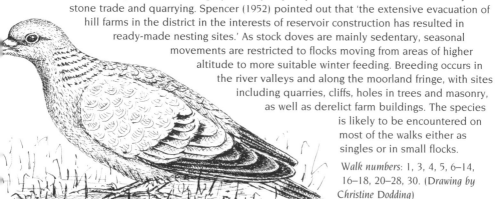

Stock Dove

Stonechat

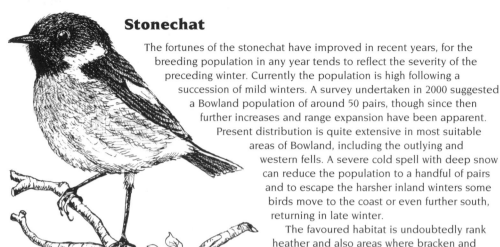

The fortunes of the stonechat have improved in recent years, for the breeding population in any year tends to reflect the severity of the preceding winter. Currently the population is high following a succession of mild winters. A survey undertaken in 2000 suggested a Bowland population of around 50 pairs, though since then further increases and range expansion have been apparent. Present distribution is quite extensive in most suitable areas of Bowland, including the outlying and western fells. A severe cold spell with deep snow can reduce the population to a handful of pairs and to escape the harsher inland winters some birds move to the coast or even further south, returning in late winter.

The favoured habitat is undoubtedly rank heather and also areas where bracken and heather mix with scattered gorse, which they use as favoured vantage points, both for singing and detecting their insect prey. If approached the bird flits from vantage point to vantage point, constantly jerking its tail and giving calls which sound like pebbles being struck together, which is the origin of its name.

Walk numbers: 1, 3, 4, 5, 7, 10–12, 15–18, 20, 21, 24–30. (*Drawing by Christine Dodding*)

The alternative, and some would say better, name for this species is the barn swallow, for this describes well its main breeding habitat of farms and outbuildings. It will also nest in other buildings and under the arches of bridges and in culverts; usually they nest in a small loose colony depending on the size and suitability of the buildings. The older farm buildings with their many beams and ledges are usually preferred to the modern steel and corrugated-iron structures.

This summer visitor only rarely arrives in late March and a few stay until early November. During the early spring the newly arrived birds hawk insects all day over the larger areas of water, but as insects become more plentiful they quickly disperse to their breeding areas, often perching on wires and delivering their simple but cheery song. Such an aerial bird seems rather ill at ease as it collects mud for its nest from a pond edge or roadside pool.

At migration times flocks composed of the young of the year and the adults gather on the wires around the nesting buildings. In the evening they gather to roost communally. Swallows used to be confined to reed-beds but in recent years they have taken to roosting in maize fields. One roost in the Lune valley in late summer 2004 was estimated to hold 40–50,000 birds, a truly impressive sight

Swallow

as the twittering mass gathered above the field before finally plunging into the maize. They are strictly diurnal migrants, probably moving from roost to roost as they head south in late summer. Their winter destination has been shown from many ringing recoveries to be South Africa, which they regularly reach by early November.

Can be seen on all walks.

The tawny owl is common in the Bowland area. Confined to woodlands or well-timbered farmland, it can be difficult to see for it spends the day sitting bolt upright in a tree hollow or on a branch close to the tree trunk. However, a visit after dark will quickly reveal its presence, for the bird is very vocal, especially in spring and later in the year when the young have left the nest. They stay together as a family until early winter, during which period the young learn to hunt for themselves and become increasingly vocal. The call of the male is the well-known loud hoot to which the female responds with the 'ke-wick ke-wick' call. Very occasionally they can be heard calling during the day.

Tawny Owl

One way to locate day-time roosting owls is to investigate any marked commotion in the woods, for if they discover the unfortunate owl on its diurnal perch many other woodland species will join in mobbing the bird, all giving their alarm notes and following as it seeks a new hiding place.

Prey is predominately small mammals, especially wood mice and voles, although it will also take small birds up to the size of a blackbird as well as young rabbits or even large insects. It relies on its acute hearing to locate its prey while its soft plumage allows a silent approach.

Walk numbers: 1, 3, 6, 8, 9, 9A, 10, 11, 12, 13, 14, 16, 18, 19, 20, 21, 22, 23, 23A, 24, 25, 26, 27.

This species is aptly named: an avian mouse which runs up a tree! The treecreeper's stiff tail lends support as it progresses up a trunk starting at the bottom, with a series of short jerks and the occasional quick jump as it searches promising cracks for hidden insects or larvae. It often appears to climb in a spiral and will climb the smaller branches, often progressing upside down, then with a quick drooping flight it descends to the next bole. Its sober colours blend in very well with its trunk and branch habitat, although its silvery white breast often catches the eye.

Well distributed in all our deciduous woodlands, it only occasionally visits conifer plantations. The nest is built in a crevice, which can be behind a section of loose bark or in large crack or behind ivy on the trunk of a tree, and it is also known to take to specially designed nest boxes which imitate its crevice requirements.

Treecreeper

Walk numbers: 1, 2, 3, 6, 8, 9, 9A, 10, 12, 13, 14, 16, 18, 19, 20, 21, 22, 23, 23A, 24, 25, 26, 27.

Waxwing

This striking bird takes its name from small patches of red on the secondaries (or inner flight feathers). These vary in number from bird to bird, resembling spots of red sealing-wax. The erectile crest is striking and this, combined with the red on the wings and a strip of yellow at the tip of the tail, makes them unmistakable.

This is one of a small group of birds which are called irruptive species. This means that they occur, sometimes in numbers, at irregular intervals. Their movements, also called invasions, are thought to be caused by the failure of their normal winter food within their breeding range, which is the pine forests of Scandinavia and further east. Most local invasions occur from November to February. Theirs is a constant search for berries, usually starting with hawthorn and then moving into gardens to search out more exotic fruits such as sorbus or cotoneaster. Under such circumstances they can be quite tame and very approachable, giving wonderful opportunities for viewing. The 2004/05 winter saw one of the largest irruptions of recent years, and birds were well spread in small transient groups throughout the area wherever berries were available.

Should be looked for wherever berries are found and potentially may be found on most of the walks.

This handsome summer visitor is rather thinly distributed throughout Bowland, usually in the areas above 300 metres. The male is an immaculate combination of grey, black and white, with the female being sandy brown and buff. The best field mark for both sexes is the white rump, which is very obvious as the bird flies away. This distinctive mark gives the bird its name, for wheatear is thought to derive from 'white arse'!

Wheatear

It is constantly on the move, flitting from stone to stone with a distinctive bow and flick of the tail as it lands and giving a repeated 'chack-chack' as it moves to the next clump. It catches flies with a quick leap into the air with aerial twists and turns to claim its victim. Other prey is captured on the ground with a quick dash and snatch.

During the breeding season this species can be found on walks 1, 1A, 3, 4, 5, 7, 10, 11, 12, 13, 15, 16, 17, 18–19, 21, 24, 25, 26, 27, but during migration it can turn up in any open area.

Whinchat

The whinchat is one of only a small number of species at home on the rather barren slopes of heather and bracken which are so typical of much of Bowland. A summer visitor, it is a somewhat stout, short-tailed bird, less erect and robust than its close relative, the stonechat, some of whose habits it shares, including perching on the topmost spray of a bush where it constantly fans its tail. It is an expert aerial flycatcher, although much of its food is obtained from the vegetation.

At times it appears to nest semi-colonially with several pairs nesting close together in what appears to be uniform habitat. The first birds arrive in late April and family parties are regularly seen until early September. The atlas of breeding birds of Lancashire and North Merseyside (2001) suggests a Bowland population of around 100 pairs, with marked concentrations to the north of Dunsop Bridge and on Lamb Hill Fell and the Tarnbrook Access Area, although recent surveys suggest that the species is in local decline.

Walk numbers: 1, 3, 4, 5, 7, 11, 15, 17, 24, 25–27.

The wood warbler has one of the most distinctive songs of any of our summer visitors, a wonderful accelerating, shivering trill and a quite separate plaintive, descending and repeated 'peu'. The song is delivered from the tree canopy but the vehemence and energy of this delivery can be seen as the whole body of the bird vibrates. Between snatches of song the bird searches for food, at times hovering with rapidly whirring wings to pluck an insect from the underside of a leaf.

It has similar habitat requirements to both the pied flycatcher and redstart, so all three can be found nesting in the same wood, although in Bowland it is more restricted than the other two. It is apparently more demanding in its choice of habitat, preferring mature riverine oak and beech woodlands with little or no shrubs and a sparse herb layer where the canopy is closed. The domed nest is often on a slope and situated on the ground.

Wood Warbler

The Roeburn valley has the largest population, but even here it has declined in recent years and the total Bowland population is now estimated at about 30 pairs.

Walk numbers: 4, 6, 8, 11, 19, 21–23.

The wren is one of our commonest and most widely distributed breeding birds. It is found throughout Bowland, even on some of the highest heather moors, anywhere there is sufficient cover to provide food and nesting cover. It is a bundle of energy, searching for its food in cracks and crannies with incessant activity and zeal. This habit of searching thick vegetation and dark crevices makes its scientific name of *troglodytes troglodytes* so fitting. Its song is surprisingly loud for such a small bird and is delivered in a gushing, emphatic manner with

Wren

the whole body of the bird quivering with energy. Its habit of cocking its tail has led to one of its local names of 'stumpy'.

In spring the male builds several nests. These are of domed construction and made of moss, grass and leaves. The female chooses one and lines it with feathers before laying her clutch. Many wrens are territorial throughout the year, defending their territory with song and threat. During winter the nests are used as a roosting site. At times, especially during very cold weather, wrens will roost communally and between six to ten birds have been observed entering a nest box at dusk – obviously a ploy to conserve heat during the cold night.

This species can be seen on all the walks.

Wagtails are rather dainty birds, and the yellow wagtail is the most graceful of them all. The dandelion yellow of the male is indeed striking, especially as it energetically hawks insects among the spring flowers and grasses. The female is less colourful but both sexes are at their most active when collecting insects for the hungry young. They fly-catch with a series of quick runs or short hovering flights, their long expressive tails ever in motion.

This used to be a well distributed and common summer visitor, breeding in all the valleys and much of the in-bye farmland. It is now a very scarce summer visitor and recent surveys have found only a few pairs still clinging on in the riverside fields of the Lune valley. This massive decline is

Yellow Wagtail

due to the agricultural intensification of recent decades, especially the switch from hay to silage production which, together with its much earlier cutting, does not allow time for the birds to complete the breeding cycle. Some pairs used to nest in arable crops but again the move to eliminate these in favour of total grass specialisation has created further problems.

Walk numbers: 2, 8.

East of Roeburndale

Start: start and finish in Wray Village or in the
informal lay-by on the right at the start of the
Roeburndale East Road

Grid reference: SD 606676

Distance: 9.5km (6 miles)

Time: allow 5–6 hours

Grade: easy

General: toilets at Bull Beck car park, Caton:
other services in Wray or Hornby.

This gentle walk takes in the lowland woodland and well-wooded farm-land, changing with increasing altitude to the upland rush-dominated farmland so typical of much of Bowland. It gives stunning views in all directions, with the Lune valley and Lakeland hills to the north, Ingleborough and the Yorkshire fells to the east, and the Bowland hills and wooded valleys to the west and south. It is well worth recording the bird species in each section as the habitat changes from lowland to upland.

1. *The ancient village of Wray clusters around the main street. Every year from late April, a Scarecrow Festival is held in the village when almost every house is decorated with an amazing variety of scarecrows. The festival ends with a fair on May Bank Holiday. The route follows the Roeburndale East road, which runs close to the River Roeburn. The first section gives close views of this fast-flowing stream.*

The banks of the river are well wooded but there are plenty of exposed rocks, which attract grey wagtail, dipper and the occasional common sandpiper.

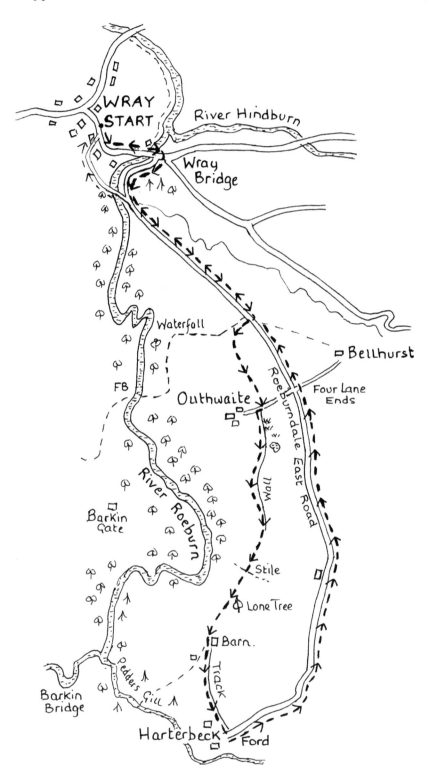

The road runs through broad-leaved woodland before rising and passing into farmland with hedges, many of them overgrown. Most common woodland birds can be seen, including mistle and song thrush, tree creeper, great spotted woodpecker and many tits. In the farmland areas chaffinch, greenfinch, goldfinch and linnet prefer the overgrown hedges and gorse patches.

2. *Take the first public footpath on the right, making sure you stay on the path that runs parallel to the road.* **Do not take the path which heads towards the river.**

This farmland has many hedges and trees with many woodland birds. The woodlands of the Roeburn are close enough to hear on a spring day the chorus of song, especially the louder songsters such as mistle and song thrush and great and green woodpecker. Buzzards and occasionally sparrow hawks drift over from the woodland. The birds here are very typical of lowland farm land with its many hedges and trees, in quite stark contrast to the higher valley which is typical upland farmland. In autumn the hawthorn hedgerows, with their abundant berry crop, attract large flocks of redwing and fieldfare. Once the berries are finished they search the grazed fields for worms, but most leave at the onset of a cold spell.

3. *The footpath now crosses the road that runs from Four Lanes End to Outhwaite Farm and continues through fields towards Harterbeck Farm. The footpath can be rather difficult to follow but look ahead with binoculars for stiles and gates and head towards Harter Beck farm.*

There are sufficient mature trees around Outhwaite Farm to attract redstarts, which will nest in holes in the stone walls of buildings. However, from now on, trees are few and breeding waders are the main attraction. Curlews are the waders of this area, their bubbling calls and alarm notes constantly heard, mixed with the calls of lapwing and smaller numbers of snipe and redshank. Skylarks are abundant, along with meadow pipits. A small tarn just over the wall from the footpath often attracts mallard, heron and occasionally teal. Harterbeck Farm also has sufficient trees to attract woodland birds including redstart, while the buildings are home to house sparrows, starlings and swallows. Swallows are always plentiful around working farms, with their constant supply of insects around the stock and the resulting manure.

4. *At Harterbeck Farm take the road back towards Wray.*

Waders are again abundant, particularly evident when a pair of carrion crows flies over. Curlew and lapwing take to the wing to engage in an aerial dogfight to protect their eggs or young from this voracious predator. Flocks of rooks and jackdaws often forage in the farmland. The nearest rookeries are in Hornby and across the moorland at Higher Thrushgill. Jackdaws nest in many of the farms, often choosing the old chimneys, although the largest colonies are often in disused quarries. By now you will have noticed that curlew prefer the fields with more vegetation, especially the rush-dominated fields. Redshank and snipe also prefer these fields but are restricted to the damper parts. The thicker cover is also favoured by skylarks and meadow pipits, both of which conceal their nests in tussocks of grass. Kestrels are often seen hovering, searching for prey, and they too prefer the thicker, vegetated areas, which obviously suits the small mammals on which they primarily prey.

By contrast almost all the lapwing are found on the more improved fields, where they nest in open situations. Pied wagtails also prefer the short-grazed areas where insects can be easily obtained. June sees the flocks of starlings moving onto the grazed fields, many of which are the brown and very noisy birds of the year, some still being fed by their parents. By late summer the young ones are moulting into the spotted, iridescent adult plumage; they look rather comical at the half-way stage and many novice birdwatchers thumb through their identification guide, puzzled by this strange looking bird!

5. *Pass over the second cattle grid and take the road back to Wray.*

Waders are still very much in evidence. Stone walls are very much a feature of this upland farmland, and are often used as perches by birds, so it is well worth scanning them from time to time. Pipits, wagtails, redstart, finches and flycatchers visit them regularly. Of the waders, redshank, snipe and, less frequently, curlew use them, especially when they have young. Walls provide nest sites for several species, especially pied wagtail, wheatear and redstart and, where there is woodland nearby, tits use them regularly.

Light up the beacon

Tree Pipits.

CD.

Start:	starts and finishes at Bowland Visitor Centre car park, Beacon Fell
Grid reference:	SD 565426
Distance:	5km (3.1 miles)
Time:	allow 2–3 hours
Grade:	easy
General:	parking, toilet and refreshment facilities at Bowland Visitor Centre.

Beacon Fell Country Park is an area of rough moorland and coniferous woodland covering 271 acres, situated at the heart of the Forest of Bowland; it was designated a country park in 1970. The fell rises to a height of 266 metres (873ft) and is isolated from the western Bowland fells. The Country Park attracts approximately 230,000 visitors each year, a magnet for outdoor enthusiasts and walkers. Full details of the range of walks around the fell may be obtained from the Visitor Centre.

The diverse habitat includes open moorland, farmland, meadowland and an attractive tarn, which has been designated a Biological Heritage Site where up to eleven species of odanata (dragonfly and damselfly), including common hawker, brown hawker, southern hawker, four spotted chaser and black darter, may be seen. Around the tarn in late spring is a profusion of heath spotted orchids. On striking off for the summit keep an eye on the ground flora of

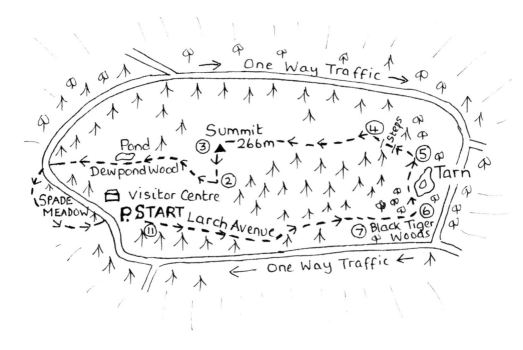

heather, crowberry, cranberry and bilberry. Careful examination will reveal one or two surprises, including bog asphodel, common cow-wheat and sheepsbit. Mammals include in descending size roe deer, fox, brown hare, rabbit, stoat, weasel and bank vole, but in keeping with the habits of most mammals do not expect to see them all at once! Butterflies include wall brown, red admiral, small heath, large skipper, large, small and green veined white, meadow brown, orange tip and small tortoiseshell. In summer the common lizard may be seen on the sandy paths and adjacent woodpiles, where it is quite at home enjoying a spot of sunbathing!

The majority of the woodland, consisting of sitka spruce, larch and Scots pine was planted during and after the war when the fell was used as a gathering ground for water supplies. Fortunately the long-term objective of the woodland management is to produce a predominantly broad-leaved woodland which is much more wildlife friendly. Management includes thinning the trees and as areas are cleared regeneration is improved by a policy of planting native birch, alder, oak and other deciduous trees along with holly. This helps the woodland develop into a rich habitat for birds and the peripheral areas of the forest are the most productive. The period from mid-April to May provides an excellent opportunity to see a range of resident and spring migrants.

1. *Our walk involves a circuit of the fell through the most productive habitat. At the Bowland Visitor Centre, collect a trail guide. Take the track via Larch Avenue to the south-eastern corner of the park at Black Tiger Wood (point 6). Follow the path alongside the tarn to the road leading to Quarry Wood car park. At the upper car park, climb a few steps and follow the directions to the summit (point 3). From the summit descend towards the Bowland Visitor Centre and take the first track right through Dewpond Wood to the road. Cross over the road and stile to reach Spade Meadow, enjoying fine views of the Lancashire plain. Turn left, walking along the top of Spade Meadow with the fence on your left. After a short distance, on seeing the car park, return to the Visitor Centre.*

The pines attract chaffinches, coal tits, goldcrests, tree creepers, pheasant and woodpigeon. Along the forest edge to the south-east corner of the plantation at Black Tiger Wood is the best spot to see tree pipit, great spotted woodpecker and occasional green woodpecker, jay, bullfinch and sparrow hawk. Tree pipits are fine songsters and live up to their name by perching and parachuting down from the tops of trees with their attractive song flight. In spring there are several other summer visitors to be seen, including garden warbler, blackcap, chiffchaff, numerous willow warblers and occasionally the familiar cuckoo.

The surrounding farm and moorland are the haunts of kestrel, curlew, pheasant, grey partridge, lapwing, meadow pipit, skylark and snipe. Whimbrel may be encountered in the outlying fields or while flying overhead calling, usually in early May. Rarities observed during the summer months have included the hobby, pursuing swallows over the rough pasture. Peregrine and short-eared owl are occasional visitors but do not nest within the country park.

The tarn was created to provide a source of water for fire fighting but is now a favoured wildlife area for gems like the tree pipit, and on quiet mornings or late in the evening, the shy roe deer. In summer do not go too close to the water's edge or you will disturb either the moorhens (which here at least live up to their name) or the summer dragonfly population. Dragonflies have been on this planet a mere 2–300 million years and the complex reproductive cycle should be given the opportunity to perpetuate the species at least a little longer! Listen for the trill of lesser redpolls to detect a flock flying over the forest with characteristic bouncing flight and often with mixed flocks of siskins. Around the tarn and leading up to the summit the finch family is further represented by goldfinch, linnet, bullfinch, chaffinch, and greenfinch. Blackbirds and song thrushes are complemented in winter by their Scandinavian counterparts, the redwing and fieldfare and occasionally by flocks of brambling.

Stop at the summit to admire the view across the Fylde plain, and on a clear day the Cumbrian fells. This location might also yield a flock of cross-bills, which nest early in the year. Flocks have been seen throughout the year but the best time for sightings is winter or early spring during a 'crossbill invasion'. A good view of the brick-red male or yellow-green female reveals that the mandibles of its incredibly powerful bill are indeed crossed. That bizarre bill must be seen to be believed, especially while attacking pine cones – the perfect tool for the job.

The walk back to the Visitor Centre is through fairly dense coniferous woodland, with its canopy producing a subdued and rather sterile woodland. It is therefore refreshing to complete the walk via Spade Meadow with its panoramic views of the Lancashire plain and coast. Spade Meadow forms part of an old landscape and a complex ecosystem. The history of the meadow shows that in 1885, at the time of a farm sale, it was enclosed in three or four fields, one of which was named Pure Meadow. Spade Meadow has managed to escape conversion to rye grass monoculture and remains relatively species rich, which hopefully future management will further enrich.

Walk 15

The Jubilee Tower trail

Meadow Pipit

Start: starts and returns to Jubilee Tower car park
Grid reference: SD 542573
Distance: 10.5km (6.5 miles)
Time: allow 5–6 hours
Grade: moderate
General: toilets and services in Lancaster.

As this is entirely a moorland walk you will not see a tree except in distant views of the valleys, so the bird species are very limited. However, many of the typical moorland species are present, with a few specialities.

Before setting off it is well worth making the short climb up the tower to view firstly to the east the area ahead of you, with the line of cairns making the path to Ward's Stone. To the west and north are stunning views over the rolling farmland to the Lune estuary, with Morecambe Bay, Lancaster and the distant Lake District hills, while to the south west lies the Fylde with Fleetwood and Blackpool Tower in view. With good visibility it is even possible to see the Isle of Man. Pause briefly in the car park to read about the seventh-century burial, revealed when the car park was built, with the remains now preserved in Lancaster Museum.

1. *The track is quite well marked and follows the fence line of the access area.*

The path to the large stone marker post on the south of the fence passes mainly through grassland and rush and is almost devoid of heather. However, a quick visual comparison of the vegetation either side of the fence reveals some marked differences. To the south of the fence on the Duke of Westminster's Abbeystead estate there is only light sheep grazing, while within the

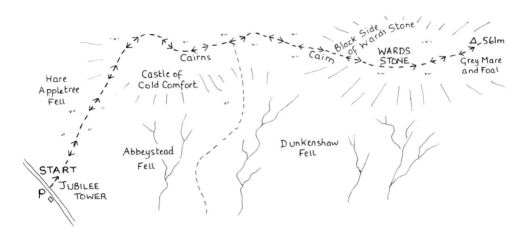

Access Area the grazing is much more intense and the difference shows. During the breeding season from mid-March to July, the three commonest birds – meadow pipit, curlew and red grouse – are often visible from the car park. Meadow pipits are abundant, parachuting as they sing their simple song. Curlews here prefer the heavier grazed area while the wetter areas support redshank and snipe. Although red grouse are considered birds of heather areas they regularly visit and breed in the grassland areas, although heather is available nearby. The abundance of meadow pipits attracts cuckoos, which often perch on the fence where they are regularly mobbed by small groups of pipits, objecting to their parasitic life style. Skylarks also prefer the grass areas and are quite abundant. Reed buntings can be found around the well-vegetated, wet flushes, singing their simple ditty from the tops of the highest rushes.

2. *Continue to follow the track to the step stile over the Access Area boundary fence.*

The contrasting vegetation either side of the fence is even more marked here. In places the heather stops abruptly at the fence, a testimony to the differences in management referred to above. Red grouse become even more abundant, although there is quite a bit of flighting across the fence. The metal plates on the fence serve the dual purpose of both straining the fence and making it more visible to the fast-flying grouse. At times grouse can be quite confiding and give wonderful views, especially on the heavier-grazed parts. Another facet of good heather management is also seen here, with periodic burning of the heather to encourage the new short growth so liked by the grouse. This practice also helps other species and golden plover are usually found in recently burnt areas. By contrast, whinchat, stonechat, merlin and short–eared owl prefer the longer heather. Keep a watchful eye out for

Bowland's star raptor, the hen harrier, which can turn up anywhere on the moorland, especially when searching for prey for its young during late May to early July.

3. *The path now crosses the boundary of the Access Area by a stile. Follow the Access Strip path with its marker cairns right to the high point of Wards Stone, which is marked by a cairn and a trig point.*

Many of the moorland species already mentioned can also be found here. It can be a good area for golden plover but they depend to a marked extent on the areas of short heather following heather burning, so it is best to check such areas out thoroughly, assuming that they are visible from the path. On sunny days watch out for the superb green hairstreak butterfly, which flies from mid May to late June. It is easily overlooked because of its small size and green colour, matching so well with the vegetation, but once found it is a joy to watch. The pupae emit an audible squeak, the function of which is to attract ants which tend the pupae, whilst the caterpillars feed on the profuse bilberry.

From mid April to mid May the Ward's Stone area is a well-known site for passage dotterel, which prefer the barer rocky areas around the summit. However in recent years this area has become more overgrown, a trend which started with the lack of sheep grazing during the Foot and Mouth epidemic, and dotterel sightings have been fewer.

4. *To return to the car park retrace your steps. It is possible to complete this walk in conjunction with Walk 9, returning to the road at either Tarnbrook or Rakehouse Road and making appropriate transport arrangements.*

Walk 16

A stake-out by the Hodder

Chipping, Whitewell and Stakes

Kingfisher.

Start: starts and finishes at Chipping
Grid reference: SD 622434
Distance: 17.5km (11 miles)
Time: allow 7 hours
Grade: moderate
General: parking, toilet and refreshment facilities at
Chipping and Whitewell.

This is a lovely walk beginning at Chipping and embracing woodlands, open fields, wet grasslands, rough pasture and the long-lost deer parks at Leagram and Whitewell. We pass the picturesque hamlet of Dinkling Green and the popular Inn at Whitewell. Further along, a late-Tudor farmhouse known as Stakes is prominently situated on the banks of the Hodder. Stakes provides an opportunity for a patient wait for the kingfisher, surely one of our most beautiful birds. A novelty of the walk is crossing the rivers Hodder and Loud using three sets of stepping stones. However, it should be borne in mind that any such stones might be submerged. Alternative routes back to Chipping should then be sought. One such route would be via New Lawn, Fair Oak and Knot Barn (see Walk 18)

1. *From Talbot Street, Chipping, go left at the War Memorial, past the Lodge House and concessionary path next to the road. Go left up Leagram Hall drive, past Chipping Lawn Farm and turn right at the fork to Park Gate. After crossing a bridge next to a waterfall continue along the track passing through two gates and staying close to the fence on your right. Turn right and follow the obvious track down to the ruin of the seventeenth-century Park Style.*

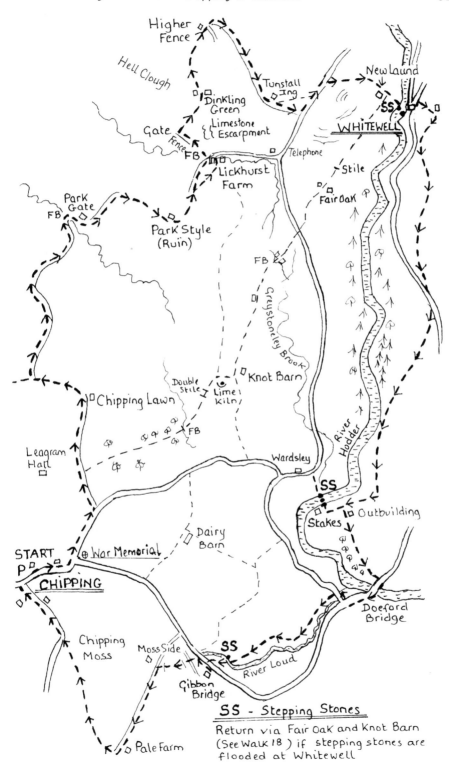

Higher Fence

Hell Clough

Tunstall Ing

New Laund

Dinkling Green

SS

Gate Fence

Limestone Escarpment

WHITEWELL

FB

Telephone

Lickhurst Farm

Stile

Fair Oak

Park Gate

FB

Park Style (Ruin)

FB

Greystoneley Brook

Knot Barn

Double Stile

Lime Kiln

Chipping Lawn

FB

River Hodder

Leagram Hall

Wardsley

SS

Outbuilding

Stakes

Dairy Barn

START

War Memorial

P

CHIPPING

Doeford Bridge

Chipping Moss

Moss Side

SS

River Loud

Gibbon Bridge

Pale Farm

SS - Stepping Stones

Return via Fair Oak and Knot Barn
(See Walk 18) if stepping stones are
flooded at Whitewell

Pass through an avenue of mature trees and follow the path to the farmyard at Lickhurst Farm to gain a tarmac road. Descend a hill to a stream and leave the road by crossing the footbridge and stile. Go up the hill through a gateway. Follow the way markers downhill, with the fence on your left, turning right at the fence at the bottom of the hill to gain a track leading to Dinkling Green.

Chipping and other picturesque villages of Bowland come alive in summer, not only to people but also to the sight and sound of the truly aerial swift flying into the roof voids of ancient buildings. The incessant cooing of collared doves is now a permanent feature of the village and as we cross Chipping brook the raucous calls of rooks draw attention to the small rookery in the centre of the village. The former deer park at Leagram is today frequented by a magnificent herd of a rare breed of white cattle. Flocks of jackdaw are ever present here, whilst the area also attracts carrion crows and more appealing species such as the mistle thrush, lapwing and curlew.

At Park Gate survey the woodlands and waterfall from the bridge in what is a delightful setting for seeing a selection of the 'usual suspects', not forgetting the redstarts in the woodland and grey wagtail on the stream. The pasture and rough grazing land on the first part of the walk supports brown hare, kestrel, sparrow hawk, pheasant, stock dove, meadow pipit, skylark, pied wagtail and reed bunting. Redstarts and cuckoo may be located during late April in Hell Clough and Dinkling Green Brook where fairly sparse woodland extends up the side of Fair Oak Fell. Pied flycatchers occasionally sing along woodland close to Park Gate and Lickhurst Farm.

Dinkling Green deserves a short break to check the date stones and architectural features on the buildings of this delightful eighteenth-century hamlet which occupies the site of a late medieval settlement. House sparrows, swallows and starlings take up residence in the old farm buildings and nearby, kingfishers may be seen on the stream. During October, flocks of fieldfares and redwings, often gather in very large numbers in trees and hedgerows close to Lickhurst Farm and indeed throughout suitable areas of Bowland.

2. *From Dinkling Green go through a small gate between a garden wall and a farm and cross the field. Go over the stile to the left of the gateway and follow the fence to a footbridge on the right. Cross the bridge to Higher Fence and enter the farmyard . Follow the lane uphill close to limestone knolls and caves to Tungstall Ings and beyond to the unclassified road linking Burholme Bridge with Chipping. Turn left on the road and look for the footpath sign on the right in order to reach New Laund Farm. Leave New Laund and descend to the River Hodder. Cross the stepping stones to reach Whitewell.*

The undulating escarpments of the Hodder valley and a mosaic of open country at Whitewell provide perfect habitat for the buzzard, which may be seen rising on thermals and announcing themselves with a characteristic mewing call. This raptor will be likely focussed on the next meal of rabbit, small mammal or even carrion – whatever takes its fancy on today's menu! In winter, fieldfares and redwings are plentiful and flocks of chaffinches should be checked for any white rumps to identify bramblings, which often integrate with the flocks on either side of the Whitewell gorge, especially during good beech mast winters.

3. *From Whitewell village hall go up the road towards Cowark and after a short distance go up the steps on the right. Turn right along the track just below the house and head towards the corner of a field. Go through a gate and a kissing gate, while walking parallel to the Hodder gorge on the right. Follow the footpath across fields to emerge onto the main road. Go over a stile on the opposite side of the main road. Cross the field on a left diagonal and follow the fence to a stile at the corner of a wood. Follow the track downwards with the Hodder on the right, and on to a wooded high escarpment then veer left to climb the hillside. Go through a gate onto a farm lane and turn right to reach Stakes Farm.*

Here there is an option to cross via the stepping stones and return to Chipping via roads to Knott Barn or via Doeford Bridge. If they are slippery and partially submerged, don't attempt to cross. Wait until reaching the other side before recommencing serious birdwatching! If returning via Knott Barn, cross the stepping stones and walk the short distance onto the road to reach Wardsley. Turn left on the unclassified road and fork right at the next junction. After the double bend sign, turn right to go up the track-way by the side of the converted barn, then follow the track up to Knott Barn then follow the directions given for Walk 18 to reach Chipping.

The walk to Stakes is likely to turn up redstart, green woodpecker, buzzard, stock dove, wood pigeon and oystercatcher. Just before reaching Stakes check out the old stone wall on the left for the locally uncommon rusty back fern growing amongst a colony of maidenhair, spleenwort and wall rue. The Latin inscription over the door lintel at Stakes Farm has intrigued many a walker. In case you have cause to wonder, a rough translation is, 'Now this is mine: Soon this is others: Afterwards whose I know not: Nobody is born for himself.' On the river there have been isolated reports of otter sightings in recent years. The otter may be making a comeback in the Hodder valley but as for your chances of seeing one – ha! Stakes Farm is, however, an excellent place to look out for the kingfisher. The supporting cast includes dipper, common sandpiper and grey wagtail, all regularly seen at Stakes.

In the past, several of these walks have received scant attention from birdwatchers, yet all have the potential to turn up rarer species. During 2003/4 a great grey shrike was seen on bushes between the stepping stones and Wardsley. The 'Chipping Shrike' is, however, elusive and rumour has it that one has a better chance of ticking the ghost of Leagram – apparently seen quite regularly! Let us hope that this rare shrike comes back to haunt the district in future winters.

4. *At Stakes the preferred (if the stones are submerged) and arguably more inter-esting return walk is described via Doeford Bridg,e the River Loud and Leagram Moss. Retrace your steps carefully by going over the stepping stones. Walk just a few metres east of Stakes to a gate on the right near an outbuilding. Follow the way-markers across fields onto the road at Doeford Bridge. Take the first turning on the right leading to Little Bowland. Cross over the River Loud and take the public footpath on the left immediately thereafter. Follow the path alongside the north bank of the River Loud and later cross the river by using yet another set of stepping stones to emerge on the road to Chipping at Gibbon Bridge.* Turn right and walk a short distance to the second public footpath sign on the left, adjacent to a house. Walk west, diagonally right to a stile/fence between two trees, cross the next field to a stile just ahead of Moss Side Farm and emerge onto a concrete road. Walk left along the concrete road as far as Pale Farm Cottage. Look for the stile on the right and walk across the edge of a field with an avenue of trees on the left to a stile next to a brook. Cross over several fields and stiles with Leagram Moss on the right. Reaching a stile on the right, veer left across a field to the bridge over Chipping Brook and emerge onto the main road at Town End, Chipping.*

At Doeford Bridge there is another chance to see goosander, dipper and grey wagtail. The kingfisher may also be located through its high-pitched 'zeeee' call. The River Loud, a tributary of the Hodder, is different in character and has the distinction of flowing in an easterly direction. Commencing the walk along the north bank look out for the interesting ground flora where spring violets grow along with a profusion of early purple orchids, bluebells, wood and water avon, and primroses. A wide range of birds is represented along the river and in the adjacent woods and copses, by kingfisher, heron, pied and grey wagtail, swallow, swift, redstart, sparrow hawk, stock dove, wood pigeon, tawny owl, great spotted woodpecker, blackbird, song thrush, mistle thrush, robin, wren, dunnock, garden warbler, lesser whitethroat, blackcap, garden warbler, chiffchaff, willow warbler, goldcrest, tree creeper, nuthatch, jay, jackdaw, chaffinch, greenfinch and goldfinch.

* If these stones are submerged, seek an alternative direct return route by road, such as via Knott Barn described earlier.

Over the fence to the right of the footpath is Leagram Moss, a pre-dominantly wet grassland habitat. Please treat this sensitive site with care and do not encroach onto the moss by leaving the footpath. The moss has established itself as a haunt of lapwing, snipe, curlew, redshank, oyster-catcher, mallard, moorhen, reed bunting and sedge warbler. Full credit for this important ongoing conservation project should be given to John Weld-Blundell. At sunset the ghostly outline of a hunting barn owl has occasionally been seen in the vicinity of Chipping and the Hodder valley. Together with the distinctive call of the tawny owl, the barn owl's loud screech adds to the rather atmospheric setting of Leagram Hall, overlooking the beautiful vale of Chipping.

Tarnbrook to Ward's Stone
and Rakehouse Road

Short Eared Owl

Start: start and return to the informal parking area
between Lower Lee and Tarnbrook
Grid reference: SD 584557
Distance: 18km (11 miles)
Time: allow 8–10 hours
Grade: easy to moderate
General: nearest public toilets and refreshment facilities
are at Dunsop Bridge.

This walk starts in the pleasantly wooded agricultural valley of the Tarnbrook Wyre. It passes through the moorland valley and then on to the highest point in Bowland of Ward's Stone.

1. *Take the road towards the small hamlet of Tarnbrook.*

Parts of the road follow the stream, with its attendant dippers, grey wagtails and common sandpipers. There is just enough woodland to support a good selection of woodland birds, including redstart and at times pied flycatcher. Goldfinch, greenfinch and swallow are well represented round Tarnbrook. Flocks of lesser black-backed gulls, with smaller numbers of herring gulls, regularly feed and roost in the fields. Most are probably 'off-duty' birds from the large colony high on the moors. They share the fields with lapwing and curlew, which rather resent their presence.

2. *Ignore the first footpath sign on the left. Go through the gated cluster of houses and farms and through the gate on to the moorland. Follow the Land Rover track up the hillside and away from the stream.*

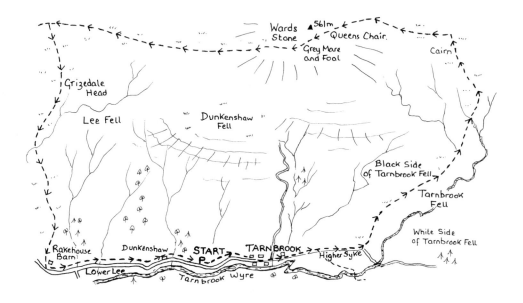

The path passes through typical upland Bowland scenery. The commonest birds in this habitat are red grouse, meadow pipit, skylark and curlew. The rather open valley, just past the clump of Scots pines, should be scanned for stonechat and, higher up the slopes, whinchat, which appear to favour the bracken-covered lower slopes with their scattered trees and bushes, while stonechat prefer the areas of longer heather, although there is often overlap between these two closely related species, as they both nest in thick herbage. The other 'chat', the wheatear, can also be seen on the moorland but is commoner on the more stony areas higher up the valley because they nest in holes in the ground, including rabbit burrows. The rock-strewn area is also good ring ouzel habitat, while meadow pipits are abundant during the breeding season and occur in large passage flocks right up to early October. Ringing has shown that almost all the large British population winter in France and Iberia, while most of our wintering birds are drawn from Scandinavia.

If your visit is in April or May look out for the spectacular day-flying Emperor moth, so large (27–32mm) that it can easily be mistaken for a butterfly, although closer inspection reveals two prominent eyes on the grey/orange-tipped wings. During May and June the slightly smaller fox moth is on the wing, an orange buff moth with two narrow bars across it wings. The males of both species fly during the day and the females at night. The larvae of both feed during the summer on heather and other woody plants.

Throughout this section of the walk the commonest birds in the sky and

the noisiest are the large gulls. There is one of Britain's largest gulleries –
about 20,000 pairs – centred on Mallowdale Fell. The lesser black-backed is
the commonest with around 19,000 pairs, with herring gull at about 1,500
pairs and about ten pairs of greater black-backs. From April to August there
is an almost constant stream of gulls heading to or from the colony. Studies
on their food preferences have shown that when the chicks are very young,
much of the food is gathered locally, including many invertebrates and caterpillars. However, as the demand for food increases many birds scavenge
around towns or along the coast, including municipal rubbish dumps and the
fish docks at Fleetwood.

3. *Follow the Access Strip path to the top of Ward's Stone. This is mainly through
   heather but there are bare peat and some rocky open areas near the summit.*

Check the more open areas and any recently burnt areas for golden plover.
The breeding dress of black under parts, contrasting with the gold and black
spangling on the back and wings, make this our most attractive breeding
wader. Curlew and meadow pipits still occur, although not as abundantly as
on the lower, more diverse, vegetated areas. One perhaps rather incongruous
sight is that of breeding Canada geese at this altitude. However, remember
that this introduced species nests naturally on the Arctic tundra. They face
quite a challenge in rearing their young in this exposed environment or even
in walking them down to more friendly habitats. From late April to mid May,
small groups (or 'trips') of dotterel may be spotted by the fortunate near the
summit. High points such as Ward's Stone and Pendle Hill are well known as
stopping off points for this long-distance migrant. Just a few weeks earlier
they were in Africa and shortly they will be on the tops of Scotland's highest
mountains. A sighting of such a trip is one of the high points of Bowland
birding.

4. *Continue along the Access Strip path until a left turn onto the track that
   eventually reaches Rakehouse Brow Road at Rakehouse Barn.*

The star of this area is undoubtedly the much cosseted red grouse. Nurtured
until the Glorious Twelfth, it is impossible not to see and hear many birds
throughout the year, although numbers fluctuate from year to year. They need
grit to aid digestion and they can often be seen collecting this from the Land
Rover tracks, although the gamekeepers now put out grit trays within the
heather. Look out for many of the birds already listed under the previous
sections. Several pairs of stonechats nest in the deeper sections of heather
and in recent years this has been an excellent area for short-eared owl.
Towards the end, there is a greater diversity of birds as the path skirts mixed
woodland.

5. *Follow the road towards Tarnbrook, taking the first left to return to the parking site, walking through pleasant farmland, wooded strips and close to the river.*

Here many species can be seen. Pheasants are so common that motorists are asked to drive slowly to avoid knocking them down, especially in late summer after many hand-reared birds have been released. In recent years red-legged partridge have also been released and are now regularly seen in many parts of Bowland. This resident of south-west Europe was introduced into southern Britain many years ago but has only recently been released in the North West. Surprisingly, this handsome partridge has done well in our rather inclement weather, although its presence only partly compensates for the almost complete loss of our native grey partridge.

The Chipping round robin wader walk

Lapwing.

Start: starts and finishes at Chipping
Grid reference: SD 622434
Distance: 14.5km (9 miles)
Time: allow 6 hours
Grade: easy
General: parking, toilet and refreshment facilities at Chipping.

On this 'round robin wader walk' you might even see a robin but do not worry too much about that for there are plenty of other sights. A feature of this walk is that throughout there are good opportunities to observe Bowland's precious population of charismatic breeding waders and enjoy their fantastic range of vocal tones.

1. *From Talbot Street, Chipping, go left at the War Memorial, past the Lodge House and left again up Leagram Hall drive, past Chipping Lawn Farm. Continue ahead, ignoring the turn to Park Gate on the right, to Windy Hill. Here a short circular return route to Chipping may be taken by continuing along the track to reach a tarmac road and then following this road back to Chipping via the Chair Works.*

   For the main walk, continue to Windy Hill and take the first footpath on the right, crossing fields to a road at High Barn. Ignoring the left fork to Burnslack keep right and go through a gate bearing the legend 'North Lancashire Bridleway'. Cross the stepping stones over a stream and walk the bridleway over the fell side to Lickhurst Farm. Proceed along a metalled road to a lonely telephone box/road junction. Turn left here to reach Dinkling Green. From

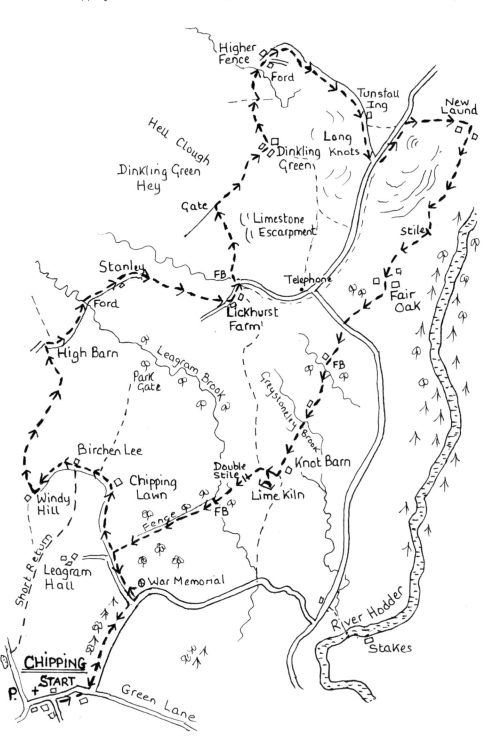

Dinkling Green go through a small gate between a garden wall and a farm and cross the field. Go over the stile to the left of the gateway and follow the right-hand fence to a footbridge on the right. Cross the bridge to Higher Fence, go into the farmyard then follow the lane to Tungstall Ings and beyond onto the road. Turning left on the road, look for the footpath sign on the right. Follow the footpath to reach New Laund Farm.

Wading birds use both moor and farmland, so good management of both habitats is vital if they are to survive. Here the lower fells, consisting of wet grassland and unimproved rough pastures, provide opportunities to witness the commendable efforts that are being made by the Stott family of New Lawn Farm to buck the national trend of dramatic declines of lapwing and other waders. Sympathetic management of the vegetation and water levels has produced a remarkable increase in the number of breeding waders, especially lapwing. Recent surveys by Gary Woodburn, the RSPB's Wader Project Officer, have revealed that populations of waders in Bowland are improving because land is being managed with their requirements in mind. Indeed, the Forest of Bowland AONB has the highest density of breeding lapwings and curlews in England. Elsewhere the picture is not so rosy as farmers have been under increasing financial pressure to adopt intensive agricultural practices. The new agri-environment schemes will hopefully give more help to farmers to manage land to benefit wader populations. In Bowland, fields close to the moor edge with small wet areas provide good habitat. Oystercatchers have now taken to the fields as well as the river to join nesting lapwing and curlew, whilst snipe can still be heard drumming and delivering their 'chip-chip' song on walls and fence posts.

Birds that haunt the lower fells include skylark, meadow pipit, wheatear, stonechat, kestrel, short-eared owl and even hen harrier. Redstarts and cuckoo may be located during late April in Hell Clough, where fairly sparse woodland extends up the side of Fair Oak Fell and pied flycatchers sing in woodlands close to Park Gate and Dinkling Green Brook by Lickhurst Farm.

2. *At New Laund the return route to Leagram is via Fair Oak, Greystoneley and Knot Barn. At New Laund, follow the yellow way-markers right, to climb onto a limestone knoll and enjoy superb views of the Hodder valley towards the Trough of Bowland to the north. Follow the hillside path, keeping the Hodder valley in view, and descend the hill to go over a wall stile. Skirt a field to reach a farm track leading to the hamlet of Fair Oak. Turn right by a shippon and cross the field diagonally heading towards the (left) side of a row of trees before crossing over two stiles onto the roadway. Go over the stile opposite to cross a field. Walk left on a track at Higher Greystoneley via a woodland valley with a picturesque stream and ford to Lower Greystoneley. At Knott Barn turn right by an old lime kiln and after passing the quarry veer left across*

the field to go over a stile by a gate in the far fence. Descend to a stream and cross over the footbridge. Follow the fence and hedge on your right along the way-marked path to reach Leagram Hall drive and back to Chipping.

The walk features many of the birds that may be seen in and around Whitewell (see Walk 12), with the route back to Chipping crossing open fields and wooded valleys. To the south west the undulating landscape features the River Hodder threading its way through the wooded Whitewell Gorge, set against the background of the long mass of Longridge Fell. The unpredictability of birding is always enjoyable and there should be plenty of opportunities to record different species. Up to mid April, findings may include fieldfares and redwings congregating in hawthorns subsequent to their long flight north. Soaring buzzards are a prominent feature over the Whitewell Gorge where access to the woodland and river bank is private. Field notes may well describe sparse woodland beside Leagram Brook, where lesser redpolls feed on the emerging buds and newly arrived redstarts sing from the fresh green foliage. Meanwhile the repetitive rattle of the lesser whitethroat or melodic tones of the garden warbler provide an opportunity to see these skulking warblers in the hedgerows of the Leagram Estate.

To conclude on the wader theme, do not miss any opportunity to describe the migration of whimbrel feeding in the fields while en route to northern climes during May. With this species their call is one of the best clues to identification. Migrating whimbrel make a series of repetitive calls, always instantly identifiable by the serious birdwatcher. The whimbrel is also known by country people as 'May bird', a reference to the spring migration of this northern wader. At the same time curlews are engaged in their characteristic bubbling territorial display, while charismatic, tumbling lapwings call 'peerrweet weet weet' (hence the old names peewit or tewit), both of which are instantly recognisable.

Nicky Nook and Harrisend Fell

Wood Warbler   C.D.

Start: start and return at the informal car park at Grizedale bridge

Grid reference: SD 537490

Distance: 8.5km (5.25 miles)

Time: allow 4–5 hours

Grade: easy

General: toilets and other services at Beacon Fell Country Park and Garstang.

This charming valley has many footpaths, allowing several walks to be planned if so desired. It is, however, quite difficult to plan a circular walk without either a very long walk or returning by road. The one described here takes in the major habitats within the area. For other alternatives consult the map in the car park.

1. *From the car park take the path by the stream down towards and into the wooded valley.*

Lapwing and curlew nest in the fields to the south of the car park. The patches of gorse in the valley are good for whitethroats and linnets. Mature oak wood clothes the valley sides, while alder is found close to the stream, which supports a wide range of woodland birds. The first part of the wood with no undergrowth and a carpet of bluebells is ideal for wood warbler and pied flycatcher, both species preferring mature oak valley woods, often with a stream in the bottom. There is an abundance of dead wood, ideal for tree creeper, nuthatch and woodpecker. The laughing 'yaffle' of the green wood-pecker is regularly heard and offers an excellent start in locating this rather difficult species. But you should not just confine your search to the trees, for it regularly feeds on ants on the ground and often finds these in the fields

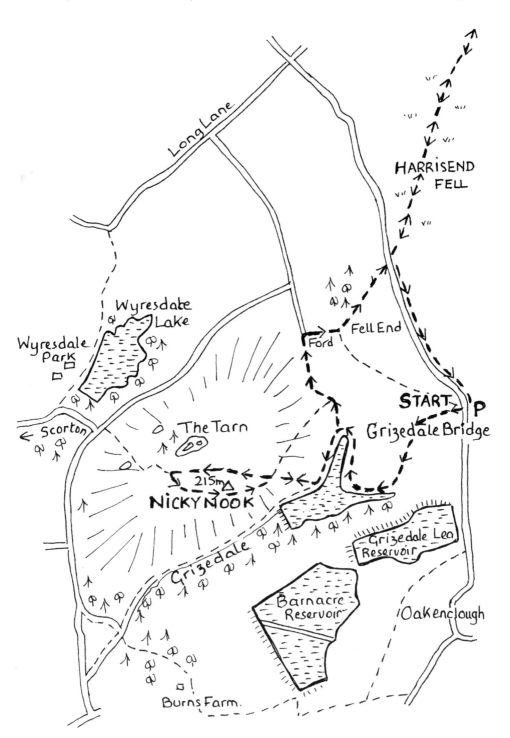

Long Lane

HARRISEND
FELL

Wyresdale
Lake

Wyresdale
Park

Ford Fell End

START P

Grizedale Bridge

← Scorton

The Tarn

215m △
NICKY NOOK

Grizedale

Grizedale Lea
Reservoir

Barnacre
Reservoir

Oakenclough

Burns Farm.

around the wood. The great spotted woodpecker is the one that 'drums' regularly in spring and can often be easily found by following the sound. It also has a sharp 'tchick' call which is used both as a contact and an alarm note. The easiest time to see both woodpeckers is in spring, especially if rival males are staking their territorial claims, often accompanied by bouts of calling or drumming and chasing. Both excavate holes in dead or dying trees, often using the same tree for several years but usually excavating a new hole each year. Our third woodpecker, the diminutive lesser spotted, used to be a regular here but has declined markedly in recent years. The path is very close to the stream in places and grey wagtail frequent the quieter sections. In dry spells the stream attracts birds down to drink, including redpoll and linnet.

Further down the valley rhododendron has taken hold, which is not very attractive to birds, although garden warblers appear to like it. Blackcaps can be sought in the small bramble patches at the edge of the wood. Chiffchaffs prefer the more mature woodland, while willow warblers prefer the periphery of the wood

2. *The reservoir comes into view and the track winds around the edge. A sign-posted diversion off the path to the right allows one to climb to the top of Nicky Nook Hill.*

Although deep, the reservoir does attract some water birds, notably both great-crested and little grebes, coot and moorhen and, in winter, tufted duck and goldeneye, whilst herons regularly fish along the edges. On the track up to the summit of Nicky Nook two species are worth looking for: tree pipits sing from the scattered trees, while this is one of the few places in Bowland where the stunningly attractive yellowhammer can still be found. Males sing their cheerful repetitive ditty of 'a little bit of bread and no cheese' from the tops of trees and bushes. This once common species is now in serious decline, hard hit by the intensification and changing land use of modern agri-culture, with an almost total lack now of the weed seeds it needed to survive the winter.

3. *Returning to the main track, move away from the lake and into the pleasant, well-wooded fields of Fell End Farm. Take the path from Fell End Farm past Fell End Plantation and to the road for the longer walk. Those taking only a short walk can follow the right-hand track past Fell End Farm, which returns to the parking area.*

The well-grazed fields support lapwing and curlew, along with the common woodland and hedgerow birds. Shelduck often display in spring on these fields, with small groups indulging in much head swaying, accompanied by the 'machine gunning' call. Our only duck species where both male and female are equally colourful mainly now nests in rabbit holes – no need for drab camouflage plumage down a rabbit burrow! Swallows, house sparrows and starlings are common around the large Fell End Farm. Goldcrest and coal tit should be looked for along the edge of the coniferous Fell End Plantation. Pheasants are obviously extensively hand reared here so are often the commonest bird.

4. *The route now crosses the road and takes in the path along the flank of Harrisend Fell. Go as far as you like before returning to the road, though the first 2 kilometres usually offers the best birdwatching. Take the road back to the car park to complete the circuit.*

The scattered gorse area below the path is one of the best places to see stonechats. Males regularly sing from the gorse, and both sexes use it as a vantage point to locate their insect food. They also regularly use the heather areas above the path. Red grouse are common above the path in the good heather areas and this is another excellent place to watch cuckoos between late April and early July. A short diversion on a side path to the informal parking area to a much larger area of gorse and willow on the west of the road is well worth the effort. Whinchats occur here, while sedge and willow warblers sing from the willows, along with a few reed buntings. Raptors are usually well represented, with buzzard, sparrow hawk and kestrel regularly seen, though hen harrier and merlin are less frequent. Pairs or family groups of raven often flight over the fell.

Walk 20

Gisburn Forest circular via Hesbert Hall and Bottom's Beck

Redstart   C.D.

Start: starts and finishes at Cocklet Hill car park,
Gisburn Forest
Grid reference: SD 745550
Distance: 8.5km (5.25 miles)
Time: allow 5–6 hours
Grade: easy
General: parking, toilet and refreshment facilities at
Slaidburn.

Approaching Stocks Reservoir by car it is worth a look at Champion Moor (SD755525). The fells either side of the road can be an excellent place to see some of the specialities of Bowland, including short-eared owl, hen harrier and merlin. In one old nearby farmstead, you may find that the little owl is the latest in a long line of tenants, so stop and say hello!

To the north as you descend to the crossroads with the B6478, there is a panoramic view of Stocks Reservoir and Gisburn Forest, the largest forest in Lancashire. Managed by Forest Enterprise, it has a network of forest walks and cycle trails. With regard to industrial archaeology it is possible to spot traces of an old, narrow gauge steam railway track-bed which crosses the track and in places forms the alignment of the walk. During the early 1920s the railway was used to convey workers and deliver stone from local quarries to the huge dam at Stocks Reservoir, then under construction.

1. *With the option of a short diversion alongside Bottom's Beck the walk is along*

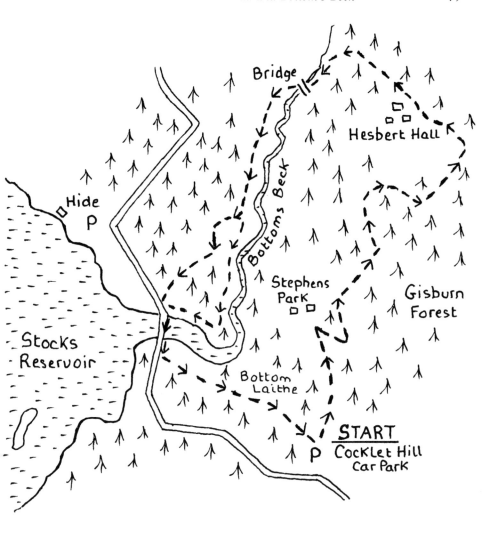

a good forest track way shared by cyclists. The walk is indicated throughout by following the purple way-markers.

This is an easy walk through choice Forest Enterprise habitat, providing excellent opportunities to observe the migrant birds during mid to late April and early May, plus a diversity of other wildlife. Throughout the whole of the walk there is a good chance of seeing two species of deer: the roe deer and the larger sitka, either on the track ahead or skirting the forest edge. Stoats and weasels are common and the joy is in seeing the former in its winter 'ermine' white coat and black tip to the tail. The pools and ditches support large numbers of spawning frogs and in early spring the pulsating, dulcet tones of the 'frogs' chorus' may fool the untrained ear. Foxes are quite abundant in the forest and there are also a few badgers. Common lizards may be seen sunning themselves on the discarded rotting wood at the side of the track, but not in bright sunshine for they prefer more temperate climes with a little shade. In winter we have a different scenario, with flocks of crossbills attacking the plentiful pine and larch cones, and flights of redwing and fieldfare searching for berry-laden trees.

The habitat around the car park and along the forest road consists of conifer and deciduous woodland, birch, sallow and larch. Check the bird feeding stations for there are likely to be large numbers of coal tits, green-finches, siskins and the opportunistic great spotted woodpecker, visiting the copious supply of nuts. The scrub is especially good for willow warblers which arrive shortly after the chiffchaff, whose distinctive 'chiff-chaff chiff-chaff ' can be heard in the higher trees. These two species appear similar but the song is totally different. There is a high density of willow warbler in the scrub and they proclaim the arrival of spring with a descending collection of sweet notes that fade away after a few seconds. Blackcaps often sing from the higher trees but only a trained ear will distinguish their song from that of the garden warbler. The forest is alive with the songs of garden warblers in spring and generally its rhythmic warble is more melodic, less strident and longer than that of the blackcap. The intriguing, high frequency reeling song of the skulking grasshopper warbler may sometimes be heard in the forest glades and open areas of Gisburn Forest, and who knows, you might even see one!

The first section of the walk will be of great interest to botanists, for the deciduous woodland adjacent and to the east of the car park has colonies of the uncommon globe flower. Walking towards Stephen Park (built in 1700) there is a patch of common fleabane. Throughout the summer the flora attracts a delightful collection of colourful butterflies such as small skipper, red admiral, small tortoiseshell and the splendid peacock butterfly. At Stephen Park have a look at the other type of peacocks that may be seen proudly and elegantly strutting in front of the old farm building.

2. *Immediately after Stephen Park there is a unique dawn redwood tree on the right. Take the left fork, observing the old moss-covered tree stumps festooned with the ants that provide an excellent food source for the green wood-peckers.*

The ready supply of food ensures that the green woodpecker is commonly seen, or heard 'yaffling', along this stretch of the walk that passes above Hesbert Hall Syke, a wooded clough to the left of the track. This and the emergency water supplies are a favoured haunt of dragonflies, including the southern and common hawker, the common and black sympetrum dragonflies, and large red damsel damselfly. Listen for the plaintive call of the bullfinch and the trills of lesser redpoll. The stunning plumage of the male bullfinch is likely to bedazzle the unsuspecting, while the thin, piercing call of the goldcrest is one of the commonest forest sounds. On a gorgeous spring day, what could be more pleasant than to picnic at the side of the track over-looking the syke and be serenaded by the melodic tree pipit? Not to be outdone, the splendid redstart often puts in an appearance in this particular wooded clough and should also be listened for.

3. *On reaching a T-junction turn left to reach the remote forest hamlet of Hesbert Hall, with the unfolding vista of the forest and reservoir across the valley. Scan for raptors, as on this particular walk it is possible to see the rare goshawk, though sparrow hawks and kestrels are more likely. At Bottom's Beck cross over the bridge and leave the forest track by turning immediately left along a less well-defined track that can be muddy in winter.*

Dippers and grey wagtails, usually present on the beck, may be viewed from the raised embankment of the old railway. The train enthusiast should look for the bridge buttress that carried the narrow gauge steam line across the beck and into the site of Greenfold Quarry, through which we pass. Tree pipits and redstart are possible in the open areas, along with bullfinches, goldcrest and green woodpecker. The old limestone quarry is now botani-cally interesting, with a profusion of primroses and common spotted orchids. It is situated high above a wooded ravine with a picturesque waterfall. **Care should be taken when viewing the waterfall from the top of ravine for it is potentially dangerous and children must therefore be closely supervised**.

4. *Continuing along the track we rejoin the Forest Enterprise track to the causeway at Stocks Resevoir.*

Enjoy 'warbler alley' with more garden warbler, blackcap, willow warbler and chiffchaff before reaching the causeway. From here you can survey the water for mallard, wigeon, goldeneye, goosander, red-breasted merganser, cormorant, great crested grebe, common sandpiper, and the island with its dense colony of black-headed gulls. In spring rarities are a distinct possibility, with a glimpse of a migrating osprey or a flock of black terns flying above the surface of the water a real bonus (see Walk 26 for a fuller account of the bird species at Stocks).

5. *From the causeway return to Cocklet Hill via the barn at Bottom Laithe, where it is not unusual to see a singing tree pipit.*

The barn area is a good place to look for the bizarre puss moth on the purple willow and a likely location to see stoats, particularly if there are any rabbits in the offing. Look up for ravens on hearing trumpet-like notes, for a pair may be spotted flying in tandem and engaging in spectacular display. If there are any 'leftovers,' rabbit or otherwise, they will find the tasty morsels!

Browsholme Hall

The jewel in the crown circular

Kestrel

Start: starts and finishes at Whitewell
Grid reference: SD 658468
Distance: 19km (12 miles)
Time: allow six hours
Grade: easy to moderate
General: parking, toilet and refreshment facilities at
Whitewell, Chipping and Dunsop Bridge.

There is the option to do this as two separate walks, either beginning at Browsholme and ending at Whitewell via Crimpton, or beginning at Whitewell and ending at Browsholme via Radholme Laund, making alternative transport arrangements to return to the starting point.

This is another great circular walk through diverse countryside, with the opportunity to spot several of Bowland's characteristic birds in a historic landscape. The Tudor Browsholme Hall has, since 1507, been the family seat of the Parker family. **For the birds that may be seen around the village of Whitewell see Walk 12.** In spring the fields either side of the Roman Road still have lapwing and curlew. Be careful with curlew identification during April and May: its smaller relative, the whimbrel, occurs on passage here during April and May. The varied habitat also supports snipe, moorhen, mallard and reed bunting. Nearby, the Jacobean farmhouse of Lee House (1678) nestles beside the wooded Mill Brook, where swallow, swift, willow warbler, chiffchaff and nuthatch may be seen. In winter check the garden bird

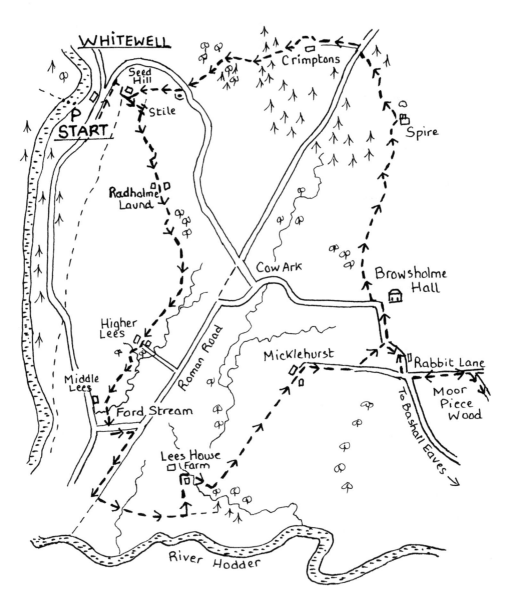

feeders close to Lee House and Mill Brook Wood for visiting finches, nuthatch, blue tit, great tit, coal tit and the less common marsh tit. Large flocks of wintering birds of Scandinavian origin, including redwing and field-fare, may be seen anywhere on this walk, while brambling have a preference for beech mast and are often mixed with chaffinch flocks close to the Inn at Whitewell.

1. *The following directions are for the complete walk commencing at Whitewell. The first section of the walk is from Whitewell to Browsholme. From Whitewell village hall take the road towards Cowark and after a short distance climb the steps on the right. Keeping right of Seed Hill Farm ascend the steep hill by going straight ahead to reach a wall stile (above a hollow). Cross over the stile and follow the path alongside the nearby right-hand wall. Pass through two kissing gates close to Higher Top Barn (left) before reaching Radholme Laund. Go through the farmyard and follow the way markers through fields to pass alongside a woodland on the left. Cross over a stile and veer right across a field towards a gate/stile to gain a track leading to Higher Lees Farm. At Higher Lees the footpath leads straight ahead, then descends left to the brook. Follow the markers, crossing over stiles on the right-hand side of the brook to cross over a footbridge leading to the main Clitheroe road and follow it left for a short distance to a sharp bend. Turn right onto a well-defined track that is the course of a Roman road, following it for about half a kilometre. Cross over a stile on the left and walk across a field to cross over a small brook and stile. Head towards the left-hand corner of a pine plantation to cross over a stile and join a farm track leading to Lee House.*

Take the footpath at the rear of the first house on the right, taking care while descending a steep bank (slippery after rain) and cross Mill Brook. Following the markers ascend the bank. Walk alongside a fence/hedge/barn on your left before walking through the farmyard at Micklehurst Farm. Beyond the farm leave the track by following the footpath indicator left across a field and emerge on the main road. Turn left to continue the walk by reaching the main entrance to Browsholme Hall. Here there is an option to visit Moor Piece Wood Nature Reserve, which can be good in spring but is usually quiet at other times of the year.* To reach the reserve a diversion from the main walk is necessary by turning right on the main road. Take the first tarmac road on the left (Rabbit Lane). At the first junction turn right towards Bashall Eaves, reaching the reserve where access is restricted to the public road. Retrace your steps along Rabbit Lane and turn right on the main road back to the main entrance to Browsholme Hall.

Moor Piece Wood has a number of nest boxes that have been erected in the predominantly silver birch woodland, which are used by several species, including the handsome pied flycatcher and redstart. Research and analysis of bird numbers are undertaken by the Reserve Manager, Douglas Bowker, in the 60-acre, semi-natural woodland. During spring, birdwatching from the road can be rewarding. The reserve holds tawny owl, woodcock, wood pigeon,

---

*   Moor Piece Wood is a Biological Heritage Site and is restricted to permit holders only. Permits may be obtained from the Lancashire Wildlife Trust – telephone 01772 324129 for further information.

wren, goldcrest, robin, titmice, nuthatch, tree creeper, jay, chaffinch, lesser redpoll, crossbill, bullfinch, and healthy populations of willow warbler, garden warbler, blackcap, chiffchaff, and in some years a small population of the locally uncommon wood warbler. In spring the wood warbler may be seen busily flitting among the fresh green foliage, proclaiming its territory. Its repertoire consists of two distinctive phrases to its song, a sustained trill interspersed with a crescendo of flute-like notes. Who could ever prejudice its return here by trespassing into its domain?

2. *Turn right off the road at the lodge entrance and immediately take the track on the left that climbs above the estate. Cross the cattle grid, go through the gate opposite and climb up the field to the right of a wood. Walk through two gates and, following way-markers, veer right to cross a field and a wooden gate beside a pond. Keep left of the pond before crossing left over a stile. Cross the field, heading towards the landmark spire at Spire Farm. Cross over a stile and follow the left-hand fence over a stone stile onto a farm track. Cross this and walk down to the right of a brick hut to the white post/stile at the commencement of the forest ride. Descend the track along the forest ride and emerge to turn right onto the tarmac road. Take first left towards Crimpton. Turn right on the short diversionary route and regain the footpath. Keep left to the corner of the pine wood and follow the track through the pines to emerge on the hillside and more splendid views. Walk down the hill to the right of the plantation and cross over stiles to reach the road to Whitewell. Pass through the gate on the other side of the road by the old lime kiln and walk down towards Whitewell, left of a plantation and in the direction of Seed Hill Farm. Walk through the gateway onto the road above the Whitewell inn.*

In peripheral areas of the Browsholme Estate, crossbills can sometimes be located during winter. Also in winter expect to see big flocks of redwing and fieldfare and mixed finch flocks of chaffinch and brambling. Almost inevitably, groups of pheasant strut about peacefully, at least until the next shoot, and sparrow hawks hunt along the hedges and open areas of the estate, where the hall is set in a landscaped park in the style of Capability Brown. Spotted and pied flycatchers, green and great spotted woodpeckers, tree pipit, redstart, cuckoo, tawny owl, jay, raven, wood pigeon, reed bunting, curlew, nuthatch, tree creepers, goldcrests and siskins are all possibilities, while the melodic tones of the blackbird, song thrush and mistle thrush enhance the overall atmosphere.

On the higher ground, cuckoo, snipe, curlew, meadow pipit, sparrow hawk, peregrine, barn owl, tawny owl, short-eared owl and kestrel may be seen over these lonely Bowland moors near to Crimpton's Farm. Leaving the conifer plantation, where goldcrest, siskin, chaffinch and coal tit all typically occur, you gain good views of the Hodder valley. Take a short break to enjoy the view before descending to Raven Scar plantation, where you can still delight in the glorious sounds of skylarks ascending in full song and dropping like a stone, and drumming snipe, ascending and descending over rushy fields. Nowadays there could well be a raven and buzzard flying over, hosted by a seemingly ever-present reception committee of carrion crows. Brown hare and rabbits are common here and the latter tends to be the staple diet of the buzzard. The unfolding changes to the landscape of southern Bowland, are characterised by its legacy of industrial archaeology, represented by the old lime kilns and mineral workings we pass before reaching Whitewell.

Kestrel.

Walk 22

Abbeystead Lake

Great Crested Grebe   C.D.

Start: start and return at the informal car park near
Stoops Bridge, Abbeystead

Grid reference: SD 564544

Distance: 4.5 km (3 miles)

Time: allow 2–3 hours

Grade: easy

General: nearest public toilets and refreshment facilities
are at Dunsop Bridge.

This attractive walk circumnavigates the reservoir, passing through mature and wet woodland, open fields and the picturesque village of Abbeystead. Although the circular walk is rather short it is possible to extend it by going up or downstream on the River Wyre.

1. *The path follows the clearly marked Wyre Way alongside the river and downstream.*

The path passes through mature, mainly oak, woodland with alder along the river. In spring the woods are a riot of colour with bluebells and ransoms under the trees and marsh marigolds along the wet margins. The effect of sheep grazing is obvious, with not a bluebell on the sheep's side of the fence! The alien and very intrusive Japanese knotweed has sadly gained a foothold along the river banks. Both grey wagtail and dipper can be found in the first section of the river. The mature woodland is ideal for redstart and pied flycatcher and a good variety of woodland birds, including chiffchaff, tree creeper, great spotted and green woodpeckers, marsh and long-tailed tits and nuthatch. Redpolls breed in the alder and willow scrub and are joined by siskin in winter. Buzzards often pass overhead giving their mewing call, while the harsh call of the raven announces its presence. The woodland path offers

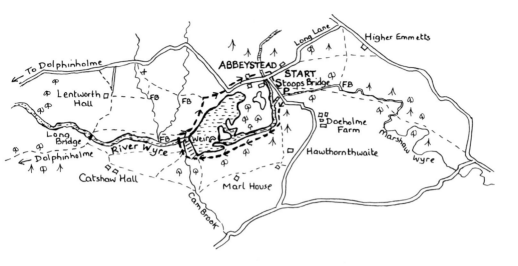

brief but rather tantalising views of the wetland through gaps in the trees; however, there are better views ahead.

2. *The area around the dam and spillway usually provides excellent bird-watching. By taking a very short and well-used diversion to the right of the main track at the start of the dam wall, it is possible to get excellent views over the lake. By standing or sitting quietly at this viewing point it is possible to see the lake, the fringing vegetation of aquatic plants and scrub and the excellent view over the spillway and down the river.*

With expanses of both deep and shallow water, the lake attracts an attractive variety of birds, the most obvious being mute swan, grey lag and Canada geese, all of which breed around the lake. One or two pairs of great crested grebe are also regular breeders. Always a joy to watch, this attractive species is easy to identify, with their erectile ear tufts and frill of summer plumage making them so distinctive. In spring they have elaborate courtship rituals, including much bill fencing and mutual head shaking, often accompanied by raucous calling. The most elaborate display is known as the weed or penguin dance: both birds dive and bring up weed, approach each other and rise onto the water so that their breasts touch, maintaining this position for a few seconds before sinking back into the water. This truly spectacular behaviour can be difficult to see but is unforgettable. Little grebe also breed, though they can be quite secretive, and often the first clue to their presence is their rippling trill call. Other breeding waterfowl include several pairs of mallard, tufted duck, coot and moorhen. Red-breasted merganser, teal and shelduck have bred in some years and are usually present in spring. Common sand-piper and oystercatcher breed on the exposed shoreline, while sedge warblers and reed bunting can be found in the extensive areas of aquatic vegetation and willow scrub. At times numbers of the three regular gull species – black-headed, lesser black-backed and herring – visit the lake to drink or bathe. Herons are regular fishers in the shallows. Under certain weather conditions, usually when colder weather means insects are hard to find elsewhere, large numbers of swifts, swallows, sand and house martins, and swifts hawk emerging insects over the water.

In winter, numbers of wildfowl are regular, including teal, pochard, tufted duck, goldeneye and goosander, while snipe may be seen along muddy margins. Migrant waders such as greenshank, whimbrel, green sandpiper and ruff have been recorded in spring and late summer.

The spillway and river provide ideal conditions for both grey wagtail and dipper, the former regularly offering excellent views on the stone work and banks above the dam. The dipper normally prefers the faster-flowing water. With views from above, this is an excellent place to watch the feeding habits of this attractive and unique species, which both walks and dives into the water, quickly submerging and using its wings to swim underwater after its aquatic prey. Kingfishers occur at times but have not been proved to breed in recent years. Don't forget to scan the trees for woodland birds, as many of the ones seen in the first section occur here also, along with the spotted flycatcher. This is also an excellent place to watch for dragon and damsel flies.

3. *Crossing the river by the footbridge, follow the tarmac road then the sign-posted footpath through the fields, keeping as close as possible to the trees fringing the lake. The footpath eventually joins the road where a right turn takes you through the hamlet of Abbeystead, returning to the parking place.*

This section produces mainly woodland birds. The mature trees and scrub around the lake and along the road support good numbers at any time of the year, including chiffchaff, blackcap, garden warbler and both of the common woodpeckers. Look out in the gardens and buildings in Abbeystead for swallows, house martins and spotted flycatchers. In winter, well-stocked garden feeders attract a host of tits and finches.

4. *It is possible to extend the walk by following the Wyre Way footpath either upstream from the parking place or downstream from below the dam and spillway. Both tracks are well used and signposted and pass through attractive riverine habitats.*

Either of these extensions increases the chances of seeing many of the birds listed in section one. Upstream is probably best for pied flycatchers and redstart, while both provide excellent opportunities to see typical river birds, especially dipper, grey wagtail and common sandpiper.

Walk 23

A trail along the Brock valley

Dipper.

Start: starts and finishes at Brockmill (Higher Brock Bridge) car park

Grid reference: SD 548432

Distance: 5 km (3 miles)

Time: Allow 3 hours (7 hours for the two walks combined)

Grade: easy

General: nearest toilets and refreshment facilities at Tootle Hall, SD 557452 (see map).

Over 100 years ago there were few roads and the hills of the Forest of Bowland were almost inaccessible. One disgruntled soul, John Watson of Slaidburn, wrote, 'Oh Bowland, thy roads are infamous, thy people's manners worse, to live amongst they hills, is a most grievous curse'. Our choice of walks has not been influenced by him, for it is the birds that provide the interest and they tend to live in the finest of places. In this walk we experience the River Brock, which has its source in a vast amphitheatre of the Bowland hills between Fairsnape Fell and Bleasdale Fell. Its relatively short sylvan course gains little momentum before reaching the confluence of the Wyre, and its soothing character is more in keeping with a pretty woodland stream than a river. The figure of eight walk(s) selected give good value – 'two for the price of one' – covering some of the best birdwatching stretches of the beautiful Brock valley. They may be enjoyed as two separate walks for those who want a nice morning or afternoon walk, or as a day walk combining the two. We begin and end at Higher Brock Bridge, where the car park is indicated by an appropriate sign, 'Brock Valley Nature Trail'.

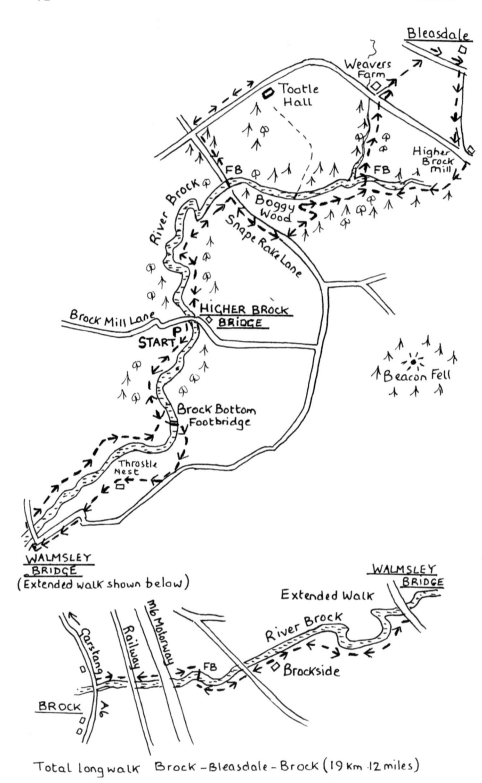

Bleasdale

Weavers Farm

Toatle Hall

Higher Brock mill

FB

River Brock

FB

Boggy Wood

Snape Rake Lane

Beacon Fell

Brock Mill Lane

HIGHER BROCK BRIDGE

START

P

Brock Bottom Footbridge

Throstle Nest

WALMSLEY BRIDGE
(Extended walk shown below)

WALMSLEY BRIDGE

Extended Walk

River Brock

Brockside

Garstang A6

Railway

M6 Motorway

FB

BROCK

Total long walk Brock – Bleasdale – Brock (19 km ·12 miles)

A further permutation is to commence the walk at Brock village (A6 south of Garstang) and walk the footpath along the River Brock, *commencing the walks at Brock Mill.*

1. *From the car park walk south through woodlands alongside the River Brock to reach a footbridge. Cross the bridge and follow the path onto South Green Lane. Turn right along the road and take the first turning on the right, indicated by a public footpath sign leading to Throstle Nest. Here look out for the footpath sign on the right that takes you above the Brock valley and onto a metalled road. Turn right and descend to cross over the Brock at Walmsley Bridge and immediately thereafter take the footpath on the right to regain access to the river bank. Follow this footpath back to the starting point of the walk.*

Adjacent to the car park is a bird feeding station with well-stocked bird feeders that provide sustenance to the local habitués such as collared dove, nuthatch, greenfinch, chaffinch, siskin, great spotted woodpecker, robin, blue, great, coal and long-tailed tits. Nowadays, this 'bait' of live birds helps to extend the local sparrow hawk population. The feeders are always worth a look before walking downstream to see dippers and grey wagtails on the river. From the river banks wrens tremble with the effort of producing a surprisingly long and loud masterpiece of song for such a small bird. In late April and early May, chiffchaff, willow warbler, blackcap, garden warbler, pied flycatcher, spotted flycatcher and the occasional wood warbler may all be detected on song.

On leaving the woodlands on the approach to the appropriately named Throstle Nest, you may see its namesake, the song thrush, in the splendid old fashioned hedgerow that is also home to linnet, greenfinch, blackbird and dunnock. In the vicinity of the farm declining species such as grey partridge, house sparrow and house martin may be encountered, along with the more abundant starling, swallow, goldfinch, chaffinch, curlew, stock dove, jay and jackdaw. On the lower western reaches of the river between Walmsley Bridge and Brock village, whitethroat, chiffchaff, blackcap, grey wagtail, dipper, and heron may all be seen, but it is usually less 'birdy' than on the upper wooded sections. The walk back to the car park at Higher Brock Bridge (east) alongside the Brock is through wooded glades past an important site of industrial archaeology at the ruins of Brock Bottom Mill. Just beyond the ruin, complete the loop and regain the path back through the woods to the car park.

Brock to Bleasdale circular

Red Legged Partridge

Distance: 11 kilometres (7 miles)
Time: allow 4–5 hours
Grade: easy

1. *Walk from the car park over the road bridge, to the entrance of Brock Cottage Farm on the left. Keep left of Brock Mill, following the footpath that takes you upstream alongside the Brock through woodland glades, descending to a piped aqueduct and isolated former farmstead with a datestone bearing the initials of a former occupier of yesteryear: 'WW 1721'. Negotiate the sides of the woodland valley via boardwalks to reach the bridge linking Snape Rake Lane with a footpath leading to the road to Bleasdale, where refreshments may be found at Tootle Hall if such a diversion (left) is felt necessary. At the bridge turn right and climb the woodland bank on a rough track leading onto Snape Rake Lane, while observing the woodland canopy of Boggy wood. Turn left on a bridleway that descends to the valley floor immediately after Boggy Wood. Walk along the footpath past Woodtop Adventure Centre and follow the river to the confluence of the two branches of the River Brock forming the main river. Here we commence a loop by taking the left-hand footpath over the footbridge and skirting the woodland to the road at Weaver's Farm.*

At Weaver's Farm there are two options to reach Higher Brock Mill. Either take a shorter route by turning right along the road with some traffic to reach Higher Brock Mill. Alternatively, enjoy a short extension to the walk by continuing through Weaver's Farm yard to Bleasdale. Follow the way-markers across fields, turning right onto a quiet lane leading to Bleasdale School. At the school, turn right alongside a plantation to turn left at the junction with the road at Higher Brock Mill. Both options now follow the same route. Ascend the rise, looking for steps and the footpath sign on the right. Cross a field and turn right, following way-markers along a path to a gate. Cross a marshy field in a straight line to a stile at Gill Barn Wood. Follow the path through the wood to complete the loop by rejoining the footpath back down the Brock valley.

This is another pleasant walk encompassing the River Brock, open areas and fields, and superb views of the fells. Take the opportunity to enjoy the botanical interest of the Brock valley, whose exquisite woodland flora is enhanced by swathes of bluebells, wood anemone, barren strawberry, dog's mercury, ramsons, wild daffodils, coltsfoot, butterbur, lesser celandine, golden saxifrage, and that other spring delight, the marsh marigold. On the river are more dippers, common sandpipers, heron, grey and pied wagtail. By January the mistle thrush sings as a harbinger of spring, for it is an early nester and is also known as the stormcock for braving the elements in fine style. By early May the deciduous trees and glades of the Brock valley come alive with the songs of wood warbler, willow warbler, blackcap, garden warbler, chiffchaff, tree creeper, pied flycatcher, redstart and the variable repertoire of the nuthatch. Alas, it is also home to the alien grey squirrel, originally introduced into the British Isles from North America at the end of the nineteenth century and now well established throughout northern England.

Boggy Wood is an excellent place to see a range of the valley's birds and to enjoy the cacophony of song. Seize the opportunity to listen for bird songs during early May and test your skills in identifying them. Great spotted woodpeckers drum on favoured trees, producing an incredible sound. There have also been sightings of the rare, lesser spotted woodpecker in Boggy Wood, but this can turn up anywhere in the woodlands and open areas and invariably when least expected. Redstarts sing from high perches in the emergent fresh green foliage. Pied flycatchers have an uninspiring song and utilise nest boxes, and summer is a good time to spot the spotted flycatcher zipping out from the canopy of trees. The spotted flycatcher usually upholds its reputation, though it is the bird that is spotted and not the flies! Check out the gorse-clad slopes for linnet and whitethroat before skirting the woodland edge.

The Bleasdale area is home to red-legged partridge, lapwing, curlew, oystercatcher, stock dove, wood pigeon, green and great spotted woodpecker, buzzard, kestrel, spotted flycatcher, goldfinch, greenfinch and grey wagtail. Walking along the road from Weaver's Farm to Higher Brock Mill, the hedgerow on the right has whitethroat, blackcap, garden warbler and willow warbler. Cuckoos are sometimes heard calling on nearby Beacon Fell. Rabbits are common and in March hares may be seen, indulging in their boxing ritual to win over their respective females.

Walk 24

The Dunsop marathon

Goshawk   C.D.

Start: start and finish at Dunsop Bridge
Grid reference: SD 661501
Distance: 16km (10 miles)
Time: allow 8 hours
Grade: moderate
General: parking, toilet and refreshment facilities at Dunsop Bridge.

The village of Dunsop stands at the confluence of the rivers Dunsop and Hodder, in the centre of the Duchy of Lancaster estates. The village green and riverside attractions make it a favourite spot for families to have a picnic and in summer parking can be restricted. The riverside walk up the Dunsop and Whitendale valleys is best between March and June to coincide with migration and bird of prey activity. The walk is justifiably a favourite with birdwatchers for it is recommended as a prime spot for raptors. The diversity of habitat offered from open fell to pastoral valleys and rough pasture should produce a good range of birds and the views from Dunsop Fell of Craven, Stocks Reservoir, Gisburn Forest and Pendle Hill are second to none. **Do not be tempted to take your car up the Dunsop valley. Unauthorised motor vehicles are prohibited and signs are displayed to this effect – you have been warned**! The option to extend it to take in Dunsop Fell and to return to Dunsop Bridge via a long scenic circular route should not be attempted in bad weather. It is vital that you are adequately equipped for this walk and that the usual safety considerations are adhered to as the walk covers extensive areas of open moorland.

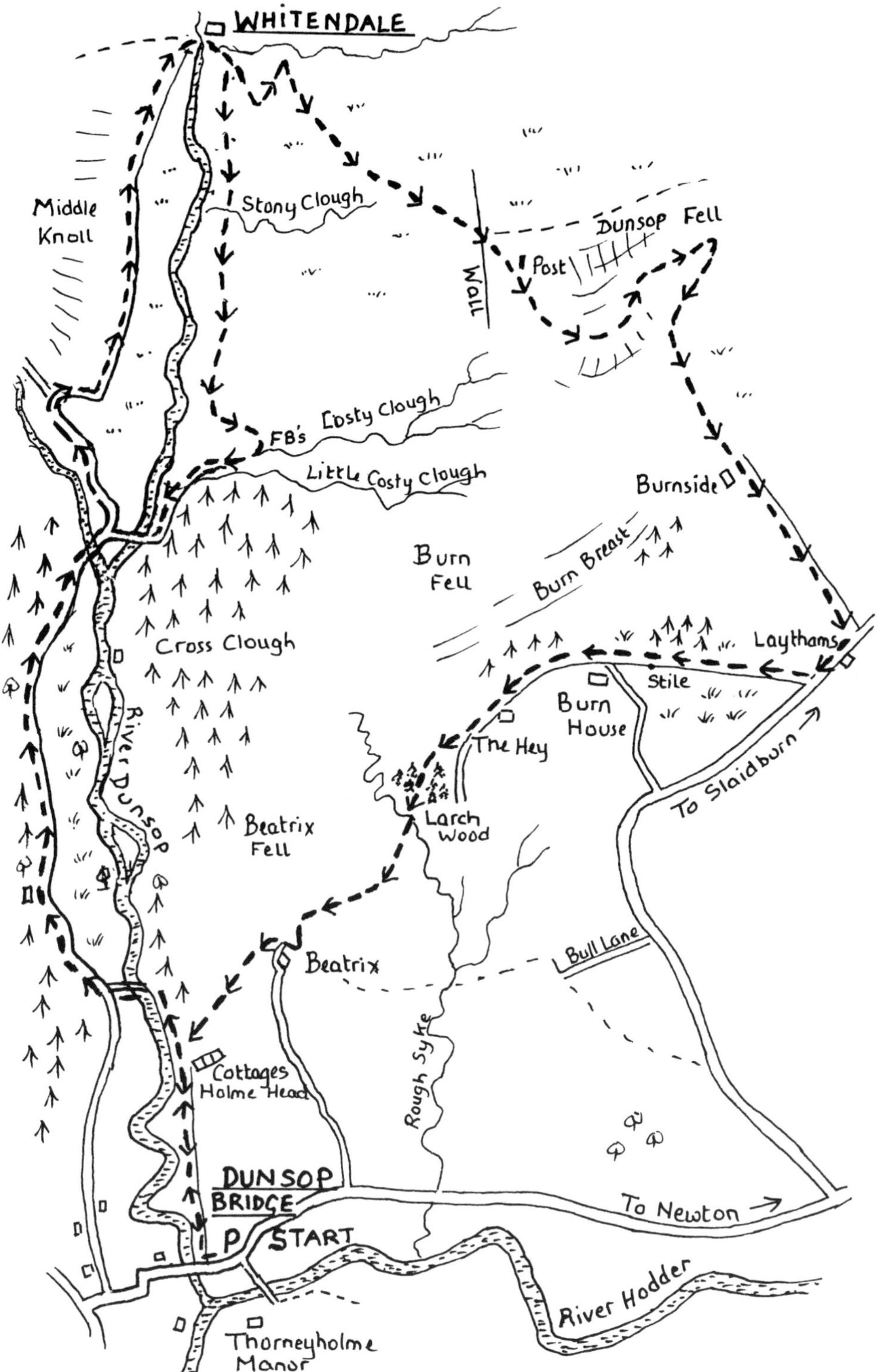

WHITENDALE

Middle Knoll

Stony Clough

Dunsop Fell

Post

Wall

FB's

Costy Clough

Little Costy Clough

Burnside

Burn Fell

Burn Breast

Cross Clough

Laythams

River Dunsop

Stile

Burn House

To Slaidburn

The Hey

Beatrix Fell

Larch Wood

Beatrix

Bull Lane

Rough Syke

Cottages Holme Head

DUNSOP BRIDGE

P START

To Newton

Thorneyholme Manor

River Hodder

1. *Walk up the road immediately to the east and alongside the River Dunsop*
   towards Holme Head. Cross the footbridge over the river and join the access-
   only road up the valley to pass the large white house on the left, curiously
   named Bishops House. The principal raptor watching point in the Dunsop
   valley is well known and is adjacent to a single-storey building about one
   kilometre beyond Bishops House.

Dunsop Bridge is well known for its domestic stock of mallards and even the
local shop is known as 'Puddleducks'! More exciting are the resident swifts
that reflect those halcyon days of summer in quaint villages such as this. On
leaving the village, the trees along the Dunsop usually support chaffinch,
greenfinch, siskin, tree creeper, goldcrest, mistle and song thrush, together
with a mixture of blue, great, coal and long-tailed tits. Great spotted woodpecker are common but be careful with those drumming sounds in spring,
when star billing is reserved for the notoriously difficult to observe lesser
spotted woodpecker that fortunately has a distinctive call. The winter
contingent of the lower valley is represented by redwing, fieldfare and,
occasionally, brambling.

Spring is the best time to witness displaying raptors and March and April
are the best months to look for goshawks. Since the early 1970s there have
been sightings of this rare and extremely powerful hawk close to Bowland's
mature conifer plantations and adjacent to open moorland. At this traditional
raptor site, recent tree felling on both sides of the road may have caused
some displacement of the shy goshawk. There are also concentrations of high
flying lesser black-backed and herring gulls that may cause further confusion
and hinder the identification process. Consequently, identification skills are
put to the test here and care should be taken in distinguishing goshawk from
similar species, including the resident sparrow hawk and the numerous
buzzards.

Even kites may present a problem of identification, for a rare vagrant black
kite was recorded flying over Whitendale during 1989. Sightings of red kite are
increasing throughout the Bowland area due to successful introduction
schemes elsewhere in Britain, while the black kite remains an extreme rarity
to north-west England. The Dunsop valley is a migration route for birds
during spring and autumn, evidenced by the well-documented sources of
rarities. Ospreys may be seen during April and May using the valley as a
migration route and one was seen heading north on 17 March 1998, an
exceptionally early date. Carrion crows and ravens often hint at the presence
of any raptor flying up the valley and their activities should be watched.

2. *Continue the walk up the valley, passing United Utilities installations and arti-*
   ficial concrete weirs, to where the Dunsop forks into two streams below
   Middle Knoll. Cross a bridge to leave the valley and ascend the hillside to

reach a road junction. On the left is the valley of Brennandale but we fork right into Whitendale and follow the metalled road to reach the hamlet. If not doing the longer walk, return down the Dunsop valley to the starting point, giving you a second chance to see some of the birds. The picturesque return footpath follows a ledge above the east side of Whitendale River and gives the valley of Whitendale a different perspective. At Whitendale turn right onto a track and walk past a barn. Turn right alongside a wall and follow the foot-path, which can be muddy and wet in places, that takes us back down the valley to rejoin the metalled road at the bridge over the Dunsop.

The River Dunsop and its environs holds mallard, teal, dipper, pied and grey wagtail, meadow pipit, stonechat, wheatear, oystercatcher, curlew, heron and common sandpiper. Chiffchaff, willow warbler, lesser redpoll, siskin and on occasions, crossbill frequent the plantations. As we reach the upper regions of the Dunsop valley where it forks into Brenndandale and Whitendale, a prize sighting such as the rare rough legged buzzard, is likely to set the adrenaline running. One was observed close to Middle Knoll during three successive winters from 12 February to 2 April, 1996, and during the winter of 1997 until 28 March, 1998. This Scandinavian winter visitor should still be considered for there is every chance that another will one day be seen in any of Bowland's more remote upland valleys.

Hen harrier and kestrel are fairly regular on the slopes. The valleys on this walk also house other members of the falcon family, ranging in size from the smallest, the merlin, to the largest, the peregrine falcon. Look skywards or along the fell side to see that master of its craft, the peregrine, patrolling its reclaimed domain of the Forest of Bowland. Aerial pursuits of pigeons, stock doves, jackdaws and smaller passerines flying up the valley are quite dramatic to watch and usually precede the victor taking the victim to a favoured plucking place. At Whitendale or anywhere else in Bowland the familiar call of the cuckoo needs little introduction. Close to the hamlet it is also possible to see the resident ravens, house martin, swallow, great spotted woodpecker and the usual common garden birds.

3. *The 'marathon' crosses over Dunsop Fell, returning to Dunsop Bridge via Burnside and Beatrix farms. At Whitendale, consult the OS Map for the route and commence by ascending the way-marked, zigzag track up Dunsop Fell to eventually go through a gate in the wall. Follow the right-hand track after the wall to gain a well-defined path that passes to the right of a gully and even-tually descends Burn's Fell End to Burnside Farm. Follow the lane, turn right on the road and proceed to the first house on the left, Laythams. Follow the footpath opposite Laythams and cross diagonally left over fields to reach a stile in a fence, then cross a stream to cross a wall stile. Head to the right-hand corner of a field, alongside a plantation, and follow the track through Burn*

House, where we follow the road past The Hey and leave it at the footpath sign on the right. At the plantation cross a picturesque clough and over a stream and field to reach a gateway leading to Beatrix Farm. Turn right along the lane and look for the footpath sign on the right that crosses fields and skirts the wood above Holme Head, where we descend steps to rejoin the lane that takes us back to the starting point.

At Dunsop Fell look for red grouse in the heather and, on the stone walls, wheatears, that perch conspicuously and flit about showing an obvious white rump. Descending Burn Fell there is a dramatic change of habitat and consequently birds. For the rest of the walk enjoy the unfolding opportunities to see lapwing, curlew, oystercatcher, kestrel, buzzard, peregrine, short-eared owl, meadow pipit, great spotted woodpecker, swallow, swift, reed bunting, pied wagtail, grey wagtail and in the scattered trees that springtime gem of a bird, the redstart. The conifer plantation at the side of the track often harbours willow warblers and our two smallest birds, the goldcrest and the wren.

Sadly, birds are not as abundant as formerly and if you have heard the wonderful song of the tree pipit, the first cuckoo of spring or the mournful repetitive song of the ring ouzel while enjoying this superb walk then count yourself lucky. Like the yellow wagtail, corncrake and other birds lost from the lowland plains of Bowland, we are now witnessing the apparent loss of birds in upland areas as well. The question is why and ongoing research will, we hope, yield positive action plans for the future.

Walk 25

The best of Bowland

Slaidburn circular via Whitendale and the Hodder valley

Whinchat

Start: starts and finishes at Slaidburn
Grid reference: SD 713525
Distance: 24km (15 miles)
Time: allow 9 hours
Grade: moderate
General: parking, toilet and refreshment facilities at
Dunsop Bridge and Slaidburn.

There is the option to do this as two separate walks beginning at Slaidburn and ending at Dunsop Bridge via Whitendale, or beginning at Dunsop Bridge and ending at Slaidburn via the Hodder valley, making alternative transport arrangements to return to the starting point.

Slaidburn is the largest village on the River Hodder and its history and ancient church are well worth exploration. This lovely historic settlement has long been associated with the Forest of Bowland and in medieval times it was its administrative centre. The curiously named pub the 'Hark to Bounty' is said to have derived its name during the nineteenth century. Until 1861 the hostelry was named the 'Dog Inn' but the name was changed when the Reverend Wigglesworth, sitting in the inn, heard his favourite pack hound, Bounty, baying outside, hence 'hark to Bounty' – or so the story goes!

The complete walk is a particularly long one but well worth the effort, especially on a beautiful spring day. One could wax lyrical with superlatives for

this walk but really it sells itself, so we suggest you just do it and enjoy 'the best of Bowland' and some of its wonderful birds.

1. *From the Hark to Bounty walk up the minor road from the pub to Slaidburn Health Centre, turning immediately right on a public footpath that follows the wooded banks of Croasdale Brook before emerging onto open fields. Cross two fields and a footbridge, followed by two more fields to reach Mytton Farm. Follow the way markers to cross over a wall stile close to Mytton Farm. Walk diagonally right across fields to cross two more stiles, a footbridge and a third stile to reach Wood House Lane. Turn right along this pleasant country lane, gradually ascending to a gate with a sign prohibiting motor vehicles. Reaching the track that is the Salter Fell road (Hornby Road), walk along the course of a Roman road for the next 3–4 kilometres. Pass a quarry on the left and beyond it a cottage to a gate/stile across the track. Continue along Hornby Road for about one kilometre, looking for the Whitendale valley on the left. On reaching a prominent marker post indicating Hornby Road (straight on) and Whitendale left, descend left into the valley. Follow the yellow marked posts along a rough track to the hamlet of Whitendale. At this point, the walk to Dunsop Bridge is straightforward, the reverse of those directions given in Walk 12, and alternate walks are offered either side of Whitendale River before it joins Brennand River and forms the River Dunsop.*

In and around Slaidburn expect to see spotted flycatchers and several other familiar species that frequent the village and semi-natural woodland that is bisected by Croasdale Brook. Nowadays that Asiatic invader of the late 1960s, the collared dove, makes its incessant calls in the early morning. This species extended its range across Europe from the early 1930s. The first British sighting was in Lincolnshire in 1952, first breeding in Lancashire in 1961 and now well established in Bowland. In the woodlands the colourful jay hides its acorns in caches and is not as much of a rogue as its larger relatives.

There are great swathes of fragrant bluebells contrasting with the pungent smell of clumps of white ramsons. Elsewhere early purple stand proudly against the less spectacular dog's mercury and enchanter's nightshade. A profusion of the differing shades of yellow lesser celandines, golden saxifrage and primroses contrast with the beautiful spring violets and delicate white petals of wood anemone and wood sorrel. Enjoy the walk through wild flower meadows that support an interesting range of flora during summer time and include the delightful melancholy thistle, common spotted orchid and knapweed. On ascending to the Salter Fell road the purple hues of heather slopes and uninterrupted views across the fells provide wonderful opportunities to see both male and female hen harriers hunting or engaged in their wondrous display. It is hard to comprehend that it has been persecuted to the brink of extinction in England and that Bowland is its last English stronghold. One reason, of course, is the perceived threat by harriers to the red grouse.

The walk along the ancient track and the descent to Whitendale also provides the chance to see short-eared owl, peregrine, kestrel, merlin, buzzard, red grouse, ring ouzel, meadow pipit, stonechat and whinchat. Nowadays the status of the latter two seems to have been reversed and the sight of a whinchat is becoming more noteworthy. On hearing its modest and whimsical song, check out the bracken-covered slopes for the sight of the handsome male whinchat. Remember that unlike the stonechat both sexes of whinchat have a white supercilium. On the upland stretches of the walk the small heath and green hairstreak butterflies are often to be seen in springtime.

2. *At Dunsop Bridge walk east along the road and fork right at the first junction to Thorneyholme. Cross the bridge turning immediately left and follow the Hodder for about 200 metres before crossing two fields to meet with the concessionary footpath leading through the hamlet of Mossthwaite past Knowlemere Manor. Follow the yellow way markers along a track to Giddy Bridge and beyond, through the Knowlemere Estate. Reaching the public road turn left, crossing Foulscales Brook and passing a farm on your left. Look for a gap in the hedge with a public footpath sign and turn left, crossing three fields to the banks of the Hodder. Continue to the B6478, turn left over Newton Bridge then regain the footpath immediately on the right. This path follows the banks of the Hodder passing Dunnow Hall on the left and is easy to follow to Slaidburn Village car park.*

For details of the birds of Whitendale and the Dunsop Valley see Walk 24.

The Hodder valley and woodlands around Newton and Slaidburn harbour many species, including common sandpiper, moorhen, goosander, grey and pied wagtail, redstart, house martin, garden warbler, blackcap, and willow warbler, pied and spotted flycatchers. There are also several sand martin colonies along this stretch of the Hodder. At the end of a long and eventful walk, it may just be time for another picnic on the banks of the Hodder or a meal at the Hark to Bounty – the choice is yours.

A time to take stock

Stocks Reservoir circular

N.B. Mediterranean gull

Start: start and finish at School Lane car park
Grid reference: SD 733565
Distance: 12km (7.5 miles)
Time: allow 5–6 hours
Grade: easy
General: nearest toilets and refreshment facilities at Slaidburn.

Starting from the car park the walk is easy to follow with the aid of the map. Simply follow the signs indicating the circular walk round the reservoir – no further instructions or directions are necessary.

Throughout this section, for ease of reference the birds and other animals are documented on a seasonal basis. In an attempt to build up a pattern of sightings we conclude with a synopsis of the rarities and a list of the butterflies and dragonflies. Further details may be obtained from Margaret Brake's excellent 'Stocks Reservoir Reports'. Please let Margaret know about your sightings by documenting them in the book kept in the hide.

The old village of Dale Head was submerged by the construction of Stocks Reservoir, which commenced in 1922. On this walk we pass below the huge dam that was built across the River Hodder to create the reservoir. Unfortunately most of the outlying abandoned seventeenth-century farmhouses that used to hide away in the forest glades and were a haunt of barn owl, kestrel and little owl have now been demolished for safety reasons. Nevertheless, this circular walk around Stocks Reservoir and Gisburn Forest is one of the great scenic bird walks of Bowland. The combination of habitat

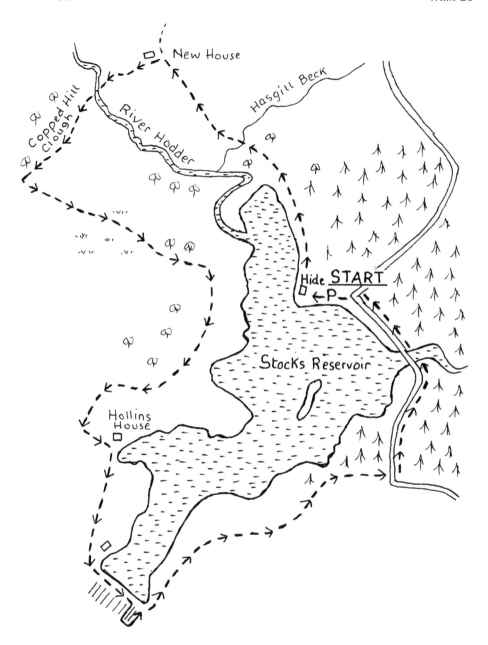

encompassing woodland, moorland, open water with islands and the River Hodder, yields an interesting collection of birds. Unlike in most other upland areas, the ornithological interest is maintained throughout the year. The main car park and picnic area is conveniently situated and its interpretative boards provide an interesting history of Stocks Reservoir and detail the walks through the adjacent Gisburn Forest. For those for whom the circular walk is too much, a hide has been provided by United Utilities overlooking the reservoir and situated within a short distance of the car park, which provides excellent birdwatching of a range of habitats.

It is recommended to undertake the walk in an anti-clockwise direction to enjoy the benefit of an early visit to the hide. Stocks Reservoir and Gisburn Forest are home to many resident birds, visiting passage migrants and summer and winter visitors from Europe and further afield. The open water and muddy edges close to the confluence of the Hodder sustain seasonal populations of wildfowl and waders.

Residents

Cormorants peak to around 50 in September but are outnumbered by around 1,000 mallard in December and over 300 Canada geese in August, with lower numbers of grey lag geese. Herons are present throughout the year along with coot, moorhen, goosander, tufted duck, lapwing, snipe and curlew. Black-headed gulls nest in hundreds on the island and several other species of gull roost on the water. The following species are also resident and may be seen on this walk: jay, magpie, jackdaw, carrion crow, raven, starling, goldcrest, wren, dipper, robin, blackbird, song thrush, mistle thrush, nuthatch, tree

Black tern

creeper, titmice, pied wagtail, dunnock, green and great spotted woodpecker, woodcock, tawny owl, short-eared owl, kestrel, peregrine, sparrow hawk, wood pigeon, stonechat, siskin, redpoll, chaffinch, greenfinch, goldfinch, bullfinch, linnet, reed bunting and occasional breeding crossbill.

Summer visitors

Certain species, such as the skylark, meadow pipit and curlew, undertake localised movements into the peripheral area of Stocks Reservoir during the summer. Small numbers of shelduck, great crested grebe, mute swans and red-breasted merganser are usually present. Oystercatcher flocks may exceed 100 birds by March and post-breeding dispersal sees them leaving the area by late August. A few ringed plovers are usually present during spring but varying water levels may adversely affect breeding success. Common sand-piper, dunlin and redshank rely on the exposed mud for feeding and are often present throughout the summer near to the Hodder confluence. Red-legged partridges have been introduced and are well established, unlike our native grey partridge that is now very rare in the area. However, one of the highlights of Stocks Reservoir is its breeding pair of the rare Mediterranean gull. During 2003 three chicks hatched but only one survived as a fledgling.

Redstarts establish their territories on the north side of the reservoir. The grasshopper warbler is an intriguing crepuscular species, often active at dawn and dusk. Its distinctive reeling song may help to locate it at the top of grassy tuft or partly concealed in a small bush. Other 'SBJs' (small brown jobs, a euphemism for difficult species!), especially members of the warbler family, are best located by song. Expect to come across garden warbler, blackcap, chiffchaff, and willow warbler and further test your identification skills in separating tree and meadow pipit. However, there should be no difficulty in identifying mute swan, cuckoo and the flocks of swift, swallow, house and sand martin often to be seen hawking insects over the water.

Winter visitors

The reservoir has played host to some exciting species, including red-throated and black-throated divers and smew. Stocks is an important haunt of wintering wildfowl and the following species may be seen, with peak counts in recent years shown in brackets: whooper swan (8); barnacle goose (16 of uncertain origin); wigeon (470); teal (1,000); pintail (20); pochard (170); goldeneye (20). Skeins of pink-footed geese are regulars over the reservoir during January and February, probably travelling though on their way from East Anglia's feeding grounds to those around Martin Mere. Around four hen harriers are regularly seen around Stocks and the surrounding area, including tagged birds originating in Bowland. Significant flocks of redwing and fieldfare are frequent visitors to the area along with brambling, which may exceed 100 in some winters.

Gisburn Forest hosted a wintering great grey shrike during 2003–4 and this individual featured prominently in the 'must see' agenda of many birders. However, it could be elusive and probably had alternate sites for its larder of wrens, blue tits and goldcrests – what a bird! Equally charismatic was a flock of four waxwings seen in trees near the hide on 10 January 2003.

Passage migrants and scarce visitors

Ospreys are a regular feature of spring and autumn passage at Stocks, often causing panic among the resident gulls and wildfowl as they hover before plummeting into the water to catch a fish. Small numbers of black tern are almost annual in May, usually when there are south-east winds; they gracefully hawk insects over the water but usually only remain for a day or so. The following species also occur, showing the attractiveness of Stocks to a wide range of species: common scoter, ruddy duck, marsh harrier, goshawk, merlin, hobby, little ringed plover, golden plover, grey plover, knot, sanderling, little stint, Temminck's stint, curlew sandpiper, ruff, black-tailed godwit, bar-tailed godwit, whimbrel, spotted redshank, greenshank, green sandpiper, wood sandpiper, turnstone, little gull, Iceland gull, yellow-legged gull, common tern, Arctic tern, kingfisher, yellow wagtail, white wagtail and ring ouzel.

Rarities

Wandering vagrants are also well represented and almost anything can suddenly turn up, from an Isabelline shrike found by Nick Mason on 5 November 1996, to a black kite seen by Derek Bunn over Gisburn Forest on 16 April 1967. A spoonbill which had been ringed in Holland in 1999 had star billing from 13–14 May 2002; five days later the same bird was seen in North Lancashire at Leighton Moss Reserve. Also there are such fantastic rarities as the spectacular white-tailed eagle that had been wing tagged as a nestling in north-west Scotland in 2002. This giant of a bird just happened to saunter up the Hodder valley and over the reservoir on 12 March 2003, to the obvious delight of the RSPB's Bowland Officer, Peter Wilson. A spectacular yellow and black golden oriole sang from cover on 14 June 2003. Somewhat appropriately, this was on the occasion of the RSPB festival of bird activity's weekend and during a dawn chorus walk. The leader Tim Melling had asked, 'Is that what I think it is?' The answer was yes and doubtless the area around the car park became the focus of attention for the next few days. Of considerable interest have been unusual occurrences of other off-course birds such as those seen during 2003 that included American green-winged teal, arctic skua, kittiwake, manx shearwater, fulmar and two American pectoral sandpipers. Is it any wonder that Stocks Reservoir acts as a magnet for birdwatchers from far and wide and that they too have become established as annual visitors in varying degrees?

Dragonflies and butterflies

The water's edge and the forest tracks are excellent for dragonflies and the following species have been recorded: azure damselfly, large red damselfly, blue-tailed damselfly, common hawker, golden-ringed dragonfly, black darter, common darter.

An excellent range of butterflies is listed below, though some knowledge of their flight seasons and habitats are needed to locate them all – small skipper, large skipper, brimstone (rare,) wall, small white, large white, green-veined white, orange tip, green hairstreak, small copper, common blue, red admiral, painted lady, speckled wood, small tortoiseshell, peacock, comma, meadow brown, small heath and, during 2000, three individuals of the migrant clouded yellow.

Comma butterfly

Walk 27

Birding in Bowland

The enigma challenge

Buzzard.

Start: starts and finishes at Dunsop Bridge
Grid reference: SD 661501
Distance: 11km (7 miles)
Time: allow 3–4 hours
Grade: Moderate
General: parking, toilet and refreshment facilities at
Dunsop Bridge.

A circular walk from Dunsop Bridge, embracing magnificent scenery and habitat diversity, fundamentally different from the preceding ones in that no bird species are detailed. The challenge is to record all the species to be found within a wide range of typical Bowland habitats. Depending on the time of the year, however, a total of over 60 species is very possible and clearly an careful approach will yield one or two surprises. Good birding!

1. *At Dunsop Bridge walk over the road bridge from the car park, crossing the River Dunsop and immediately thereafter veer off on a footpath to the left. Cross over two wall stiles and after the second stile veer left to reach a track. Follow the track to the banks of the Hodder heading towards Whitewell. Cross the green footbridge and walk right along the footpath to Burholme Bridge. Cross the road bridge and take the unclassified road on the left leading to Chipping. Take the second footpath sign on the right that crosses fields leading onto a tarmac farm track to Higher Fence. Take a right turn along a track leading to Whitmore Farm indicated by a sign saying 'North Lancashire*

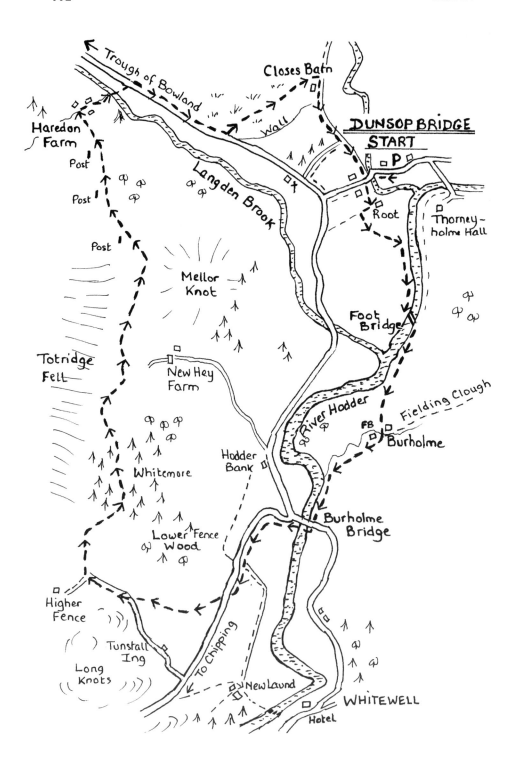

Bridleway'. Before reaching Whitmore Farm, turn right by some hen cabins following the North Lancashire Bridleway logo on posts for the next section of the walk. The track is obvious through Whitemore Forest and above New Hey Farm but becomes less distinct on the open moor below Totridge Fell. Follow the footpath north (indicated by the posts) crossing over two wall stiles to descend the valley along the side of a wall, veering right to the line of posts to reach a stile at the hamlet of Hareden.

At Hareden turn right and walk the short distance to the main Trough of Bowland road. Turn right on the main road to reach a cattle grid. Cross over the cattle grid looking out for the North Lancashire Bridleway sign on the left after 100 metres. Leave the main road here and keep right, walking towards the Dunsop valley and a farm called Closes Barn. Take a low course (south) indicated by the posts, eventually gaining and keeping parallel to a wall on the right to go through an iron gate at Closes Barn. Turn right on the road bisecting the Dunsop valley to reach the Forest Enterprise office on the left. At this point it may be worth examining Forest Enterprise woodland at Black Plantation on the right, rich in warblers and other species in April and May. A well-defined track branches off outside the office, bisecting this plantation and leading in a short distance to the Trough of Bowland road. Return to the starting point at Dunsop Bridge by continuing along the minor valley road or taking the track through the plantation and retracing your steps back to the same road, and then turning right to reach Dunsop Bridge.

The Lune Estuary

The final three walks are just outside the Forest of Bowland AONB and on the coast just a few miles to the west. The reason for their inclusion is to give the opportunity to see where many of Bowland's birds, especially the breeding waders but also some of the raptors and passerines, spend the winter. They also give superb birdwatching, especially in winter, and allow a visiting bird-watcher the opportunity to see the outstanding variety and superb spectacle of large numbers of waders and wildfowl. They also provide something of a contrast to the other walks and give excellent birdwatching at a time when other areas are relatively quiet.

Winter spectacular: waders and wildfowl at Fluke Hall and Pilling

Curlew.   CD

Start: start and return to Fluke Hall car park
Grid reference: SD 389500
Distance: 3km (2 miles) (extension by car *c*. 12km, 7.5 miles)
Time: 4 hours
Grade: easy
General: toilets and other services in Pilling.

This walk gives excellent birdwatching from late July through to late May. However the tidal section of the walk is very tide-dependent, featuring an unforgettable spectacle of ten of thousands of mixed waders gathering to roost as the tide displaces them from the inter-tidal area. When the tide is out they feed on the invertebrates which occur in superabundance, which means that the waders congregate at high tide on any exposed sand bank, salt marsh or beach. So it is imperative to get the timing right and visit at the recommended times and state of the tide. Tidal timing and heights are available in most local papers, tide tables can be purchased from fishing shops, alternatively tidal information can be found at The predictions and heights most readily available are those for Liverpool and they are very similar to those on the Lune estuary and are used in this walk. The tidal heights suitable to get the best birdwatching are those above 8.5m. These occur around the middle of the day. Tidal height can be affected by weather conditions, with a strong westerly wind making the tide higher and calm anti-cyclonic conditions having the opposite effect.

1. *Park in the small car park at Fluke Hall, preferably two hours before high tide*

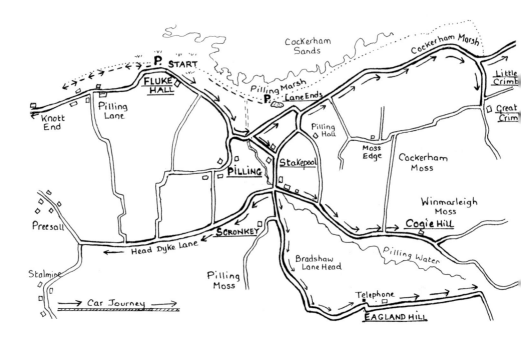

and walk on top of the sea wall to the left, towards Knott End. DO NOT GO ONTO THE INTER-TIDAL AREA. Details of how far to walk are given in the account below, all depending on tide height and birds present.

The fields behind the sea wall hold migrants in spring and autumn such as wheatear, meadow pipits, skylarks, linnets and twite. Large flocks of lapwing and, at times, golden plover and curlew, occur on these fields and some will have originated in Bowland. In winter huge flocks of pink-footed geese occur at times. They announce their presence usually before you spot them, especially if they have been disturbed. On the seaward side of the sea wall, depending on the wetness of the sand, small flocks of redshank and dunlin may be feeding. In some winters a small flock of snow buntings winter along the embankment. Check with binoculars regularly towards Knott End to watch for the wader flocks starting to assemble, which will show as a massed flock against the quickly moving tide line. Walk down until you are opposite the first substantial flock. The distance you have to walk will depend on eventual tide height, weather conditions and of course the time you set out and how much there is to see on the way out. Once you have reached the flocks, the best plan is to slowly walk back, keeping up with the waders, which are being slowly forced towards you by the incoming tide.

Enjoy the spectacle of the massed throngs, especially thrilling when they take to flight, twisting and turning like animated smoke. Observe how the long-legged bar-tailed godwit and curlew stand further out in the water and next is a great pack of oystercatchers with smaller numbers of grey plover and redshank with somewhat shorter legs, but closest are the vast throngs of knot dunlin and smaller numbers of ringed plover and sanderling, all with shorter legs and often many still feeding. Numbers do of course vary depending on the season. August to early September can be very good for variety, especially as many adult birds are still in the bright breeding plumage. Remarkably, many of these waders have travelled from as far away as Arctic Canada, Greenland and Siberia. In many species the first birds to arrive back are the females for they leave the male in charge of the young. The sanderling though is unique for the female lays two clutches, one of which she incubates the other the male tends! Birds are not always able to breed successfully each year in the high Arctic so the sanderling makes good use of those years when conditions are suitable. In late summer flocks of terns, mainly common, Arctic and sandwich, roost with the waders. All our regular land-based gull species also occur at this time.

The largest numbers of waders occur from mid October onward, mainly because many knot, which moult along the north Sea coast, move to the west coast after completing their moult. Many species start to move out in late February with oystercatchers being the first to leave. April and May sees numbers of passage ringed plover, dunlin and sanderling, many in full summer plumage. The latter has been shown to make the journey non-stop from Britain to Greenland, while some other species use Iceland as a refuelling halt. Indeed many of the birds at this time of year have wintered further south in Southern Europe or West Africa and they are using the inter-tidal areas of the Lune estuary as a stopping off point to refuel on the superabundant bi–valves and sand hoppers.

Where the waders roost at high tide will depend on the eventual height of the tide, and also on the level of disturbance, both human and avian. On tides below 9 metres, they usually roost on the exposed sand to the south of Fluke Hall car park. On higher tides they flight to the large salt marsh upstream of the car park, best viewed by telescope from the sea wall at Fluke Hall. With the turn of the tide the waders become more settled and rest over the high tide until the sands are exposed again and they can resume feeding. However the most breath-taking spectacle occurs when a peregrine or merlin 'beats up' the wader flock, causing them to twist and turn in superb unison. Despite the tens of thousands of potential prey, it is amazing how often the predators miss! But if and when they catch, they regularly fly to the salt marsh or sea wall to pluck the unfortunate victim and peace returns to the flock, although if the attacks are sustained for any period many waders, especially the smaller ones, will flight away across the estuary to find refuge. Returning to the car park it is well worth looking over the hedge into the usually arable field. In winter this generally supports a mixed flock of greenfinch, chaffinch, linnet, twite and tree sparrow, and both grey- and red-legged partridge are regulars.

2. *Another excellent view of the wader roost is available from the east side by driving to Lane End's Amenity Area (see map), which has an excellent car park on top of the sea wall. It is quite possible to walk to this new site along the road, and past the Golden Ball Hotel; however, as time is of the essence before the high tide roost breaks up and because winter days are short, driving is recommended.*

At times the major part of the wader roost is visible from this site. By walking back along the sea wall towards Fluke Hall one gets a much closer view. However, rather strangely this part of the embankment is closed to public access from 27 December to Good Friday. Both grey and golden plover regularly roost on the salt marsh just out from the car park. It is also the best place to see wildfowl, which mainly congregate in the mouth of the Pilling Water. Wigeon, mallard and shelduck are the commonest but teal, shoveler, pintail and red-breasted merganser are usually present, with a small flock of wintering dark-bellied brent geese. Flocks of pink-feet regularly graze on the salt marsh or flight inland to the mossland fields round Pilling, or even to Marton Mere and the Ribble marshes. The tide line attracts small flocks of skylarks and meadow pipits, and at times brown hares can be seen retreating from the tide. Raptors encountered regularly are peregrine, merlin, sparrow hawk and kestrel, and less frequently hen harrier and short-eared owl.

3. *During winter and early spring the fields around Pilling are the feeding grounds of up to 10,000 pink-feet, with the largest numbers occurring from early January to early March. The flocks are quite mobile and it is something of a wild goose chase to locate them. Again, driving is best not only because a larger area can be covered but also at times the car makes a good hide. The best locations include Crimbles Lane, Scronkey, Cogie Hill and Eagland Hill. For details of how to reach these sites consult the map.*

Very often the first clue as to which area the pink-feet are using is when they take to flight. With them, especially after the turn of the year, are small numbers of European white-fronted geese, whooper and bewick's swan, barnacle geese as well as greylag and Canada. The area around Eagland Hill is a favoured area and in recent years this has held a further attraction with the provision of feeding stations for wintering passerines. This excellent project, organised by Bob Danson, attracts large numbers of tree sparrows, yellowhammers, corn buntings, and at times brambling, along with many of the common finches to the two sites just off the road either side of Eagland Hill (see map). Other birds to watch for in winter include flocks of redwing and fieldfare, both partridges, merlin, sparrow hawk and little owl. If you linger on the mosses towards dusk there is a very good chance that an excellent day's birdwatching will end on a high note with good views of a hunting barn owl.

Wader Flock   CD.

Birdwatching at Conder Green

Grey Plover

Start: start and return to Conder Green Picnic Site
Grid reference: SD 457562
Distance: 3km (2 miles)
Time: 2–3 hours
Grade: easy
General: toilets in the picnic site; other services at Conder Green and Glasson.

This walk is offered with two options. A short one, Walk 29, covers the small Conder estuary and part of the Lune estuary. A much longer circular walk, 29A, includes the inland areas, with a pleasant canal walk. There is a third longer coastal option, Walk 30. The shorter option can be undertaken in the morning before going on to view the wader roost at Pilling, described in Walk 28. The Conder is the only muddy estuary on Morecambe Bay and holds a good variety of waders at most states of the tide especially low water. Beware though of high spring tides which flood the road and can maroon you in the car park for an hour or so. So always consult the tide tables before setting out.

1. *The Conder Green picnic site car park is good for common woodland and garden birds, especially when a feeding station has been provided there. From the slightly elevated area by the picnic tables there is a good view across the salt marsh to the Lune estuary.*

A telescope is needed for most birds, but the exposed sand flats attract flocks of dunlin, redshank and at times bar-tailed godwits. On the exposed rocky mussel beds can be found turnstone and ringed plover and also large,

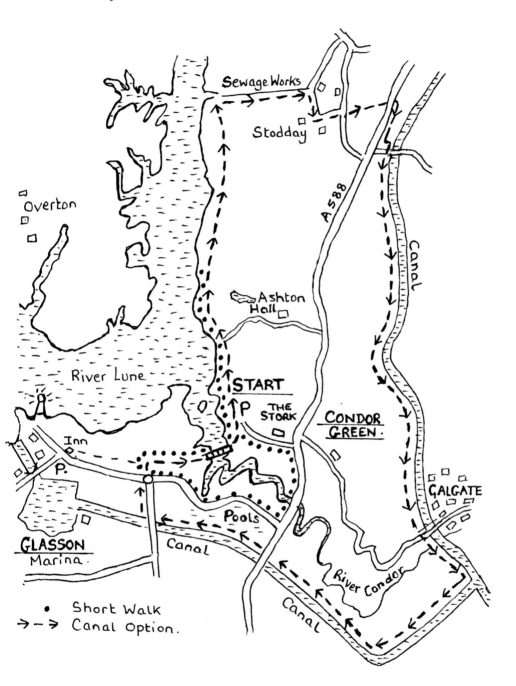

Sewage Works

Stodday

A588

Canal

Overton

River Lune

Ashton Hall

START

P   THE STORK

CONDOR GREEN.

GALGATE

Pools

Canal

GLASSON
Marina.

Inn

P.

River Condor

Canal

•   Short Walk
→ - →   Canal Option.

daytime roosting flocks of lapwing and golden plover which regularly flight inland to the feeding fields. In winter numbers of wigeon, goldeneye and red-breasted merganser frequent the channel and come onto the salt marsh at high tide, a habitat also used by wintering reed bunting and linnet.

2. *Walk south from the car park towards the River Conder and pause on the old railway bridge that spans the river. This gives views of the river both ways. Walk along the course of the old railway track then take the first footpath left by a new metal gate, which takes you to the road. Turn left onto the road and continue back over the bridge, then left past the Stork Pub and back to the car park.*

A good mixture of waders feed along the muddy margins, including grey plover, turnstone, redshank, curlew, snipe and dunlin. The variety depends on the season with the largest numbers from early August to early October. It also varies from year to year, depending on breeding success in the Arctic and the wind direction at migration times. During the autumn passage, common sandpiper, ruff, greenshank, spotted redshank, godwits and whimbrel are regular, with green and wood sandpipers less frequent. In good years numbers of little stint and curlew sandpiper occur, with a few adults in late July/early August and larger numbers of juveniles moving through in September. Pause regularly to search the mud, especially where you can look down sections of the strongly meandering river. Check also the pool on the south of the road. There is a raised platform designed to aid watching over this recently evacuated pool which has attracted many of the species already listed and little-ringed plover, but at the time of writing is becoming rather too vegetated for waders. Besides waders the Conder attracts many teal, shel-duck and a few other wildfowl. Kingfishers are regulars outside the breeding season. The stretch of river visible from the road bridge is a favoured site for this colourful species and also for green sandpiper. One interesting site is flocks of starlings behaving like waders searching for rich pickings in the soft mud. Besides the regulars already described, the estuary has an impressive list of rarities especially over spring and autumn passage periods. Black terns and little gulls occur especially in spring while common terns regularly fish in summer. The estuary also attracts wintering spotted redshank and green-shank . The bushes and hedges bordering the site should not be neglected, as finches and sparrows, including tree sparrows, are regulars, while in late summer migrant warblers should be sought. The old railway banks and path edges are excellent for butterflies, including small copper, grayling and common blue in season.

3. *Once back in the car park, walk north on the Lancashire Coastal Way past the toilets along the path, which for much of it way hugs the edge of the estuary,*

giving views all the time of birds in the river and the exposed inter-tidal area,
and also of birds in the hedgerows and bordering fields. On the short option,
go as far as your timing allows then retrace your steps back to the car park.

The first field after leaving the car park is often the best with regular flocks of
lapwing, golden plover and fewer curlew and redshank. Largest numbers
occur during wet mild spells in winter, when numbers of redwing and fieldfare
also occur. Watch out for panic spreading through the wader or gull flocks,
often a sign that a predatory peregrine, merlin or sparrow hawk is about.
Winter wildfowl include many wigeon and teal, and in late winter numbers of
pink-feet.

In early summer, creches of young shelduck assemble, looked after by a
few adults while the rest of the adult population make a moult migration to
the Heligoland Bight in Germany, before returning in late September in pristine new dress. Along the river bank cormorants hang their wings out to dry
and herons stalk in the shallows while goosanders fish in the deeper sections.

Conder Green: the canal option

Distance: 13km (8 miles)
Time: 4 hours
Grade: easy.

his walk takes in parts of the estuary of the rivers Lune and Conder, and a circular walk through pleasant agricultural land along the canal towpath.

4. *Follow the Lancashire Coastal Way north from the picnic site until a marked right turn by the sewage works. This track joins the road then skirts the village of Stodday, where there is a footpath that goes to the main Lancaster to Fleetwood Road (A588). After a right turn onto the road and a short distance, take a left turn to the canal bridge where the canal towpath is joined, and continue south until the towpath along the Glasson Dock Branch Canal is reached.*

The walk takes the same route as 3 above but then passes through farmland and small sections of woodland adjacent to the canal. On the canal is the usual motley collection of mallard, many with signs of mixed parentage! Moorhen, coot and mute swan are regulars, while kingfishers are often seen outside the breeding season. Flocks of lapwing, rooks and jackdaws occur in the fields. In winter redwing and fieldfare are regular, while a good mixture of typical hedgerow and woodland birds occur throughout. The village of Galgate holds breeding swifts and house martins.

5. *Turn off the main canal onto the Glasson Dock branch. Follow the towpath until the last bridge just before Glasson Dock is reached. This gives access to the road where a right turn across the roundabout and then onto the Coastal Footpath and north to the picnic site.*

For water birds this is probably the best section with good numbers of coot and moorhen, and usually a pair of great crested grebe. Sedge warblers and reed buntings sing from the reeded edge. Because of its proximity to Glasson marina and dock, occasionally unusual birds seek shelter, especially after gales in the Irish Sea. Under such conditions there have been records of red-throated diver, guillemot and Leach's petrel.

To Cockersands and back

Merlin.   C.D.

Start: start and return to Conder Green picnic site
Grid reference: SD 457562
Distance: 11km (7 miles)
Time: 4 hours
Grade: easy
General: toilets in the picnic site; other services at
Conder Green and Glasson.

An opportunity to explore a little more of the Lune estuary, which can be productive at all states of the tide, and then return through low-lying farmland. Beware though of high spring tides which flood the road and can maroon you in the car park for an hour or so; always consult the tide tables before setting out.

1. *Follow the coastal footpath south out of the picnic site until a left turn across the roundabout and over the canal bridge. Take the first right round the back of Glasson Marina and at the next right angle turn take the footpath towards Crook Farm, then along the embankment ending opposite the lighthouse on Plover Scar near Cockersands. This section gives good views over the Lune estuary to Sunderland Point. The Heysham Nuclear Power Station rather dominates the distant view.*

Outside the breeding season this is an excellent area for flocks of lapwing and golden plover both on the fields and the salt marsh. With them especially in wet periods will be smaller numbers of redshank, curlew, oystercatcher and occasionally dunlin and knot. The salt marsh supports good numbers of wigeon and shelduck. The embankment is an excellent vantage point

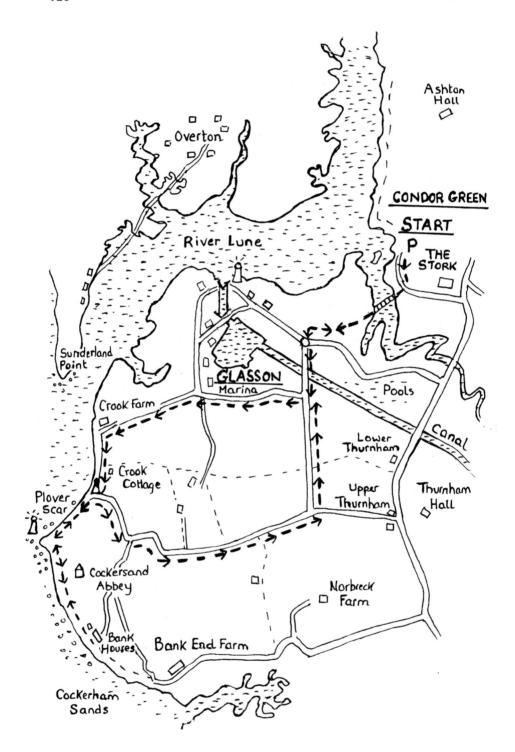

for viewing the estuary. At low water and as the tide ebbs and flows, the sands and scars are sprinkled with small groups and flocks of dunlin, knot, oystercatcher, curlew and redshank. The Cockersands area is also usually excellent for grey plover, bar-tailed and at times black-tailed godwits, turn-stone, ringed plover and during spring and autumn passage, sanderling, On the lower or neap tides the shingle spit near the lighthouse serves as a high tide roost for many of these waders, but on the higher or spring tides it is covered and the waders flight across the estuary to the large salt marsh to the west of Sunderland Point. The river channel is good at any state of the tide for red-breasted mergansers and at times goosanders along with goldeneye and great crested grebe. Long-tailed ducks and the rarer grebes have also been recorded. From April to September terns can often be seen. Common terns are the most regular but Arctic, sandwich and little terns occur at passage times. Gale force winds regularly blow in seabirds such as gannet, kittiwake and guillemot.

The fields behind the sea wall, besides holding the waders already mentioned, are good for wintering passerines, which are rather dependent on the cropping regime. Stubble fields are best and when conditions are right, flocks of skylarks, mixed finches, buntings and sparrows, including twite, linnet and tree sparrow, are well worth searching for.

2. *Return past the small car park to the land-based lighthouse, now converted to a house, and take the road inland. Continue along this road inland until a left turn down Jeremy Lane is made, which returns you across the canal bridge to the roundabout. Here there is the option of going back to the car park along the coastal path or you can follow the route outlined in section 2 of Walk 29 around the Conder estuary past the Stork pub and back to the car park.*

The fields hold good numbers of the waders already described under section 1. Golden plover and lapwing often feed right up to the road. With them in winter are flocks of redwing and fieldfare and, as in the last section, if there is a stubble field this can be very good for winter passerines. Many of the fields are bordered by reed-filled ditches, in which breed reed buntings and sedge warblers. Merlins, peregrines and sparrow hawks often hunt these fields while in late winter, flocks of pink-feet visit. The fields either side of Jeremy Lane have in recent winters become good for wintering swans, with up to 70+ mute swan and with them smaller numbers of bewick's and whooper swans, which look rather out of place grazing on the lush grass well away from water.

Seasonal Occurrence Chart

This is intended as a guide as to when species can be found throughout each month of the year. However it must be remembered that there are many variations between species, habitats and seasons, so the categories given for a particular species are subjective and are only intended as a guide. The abundance of a bird and the habitat it occupies can change with the seasons. For example, curlew and lapwing breed widely on fell farms, but resort to the coast and adjacent low-lying land in winter.

Birds are listed in the chart in alphabetical order of common name. Those mainly occurring on the coast are marked with a C after the name. Extreme rarities which have occurred are not included. The chance of seeing a species will also depend upon the experience of the observer and his knowledge of calls and song and the habitat frequented.

Key

- Frequent and likely to be encountered in suitable habitat within Bowland and the coastal areas.

- Present in only small numbers in suitable habitat within the area.

- A few present and unlikely to be seen.

- Only very exceptional sightings.

	Jan	Feb	Mar	Apr	May	Jun	Jul	Aug	Sep	Oct	Nov	Dec
Artic skua C				∙∙••	•••∙		∙∙••	••••	∙∙∙∙			
Artic tern C				∙∙••	••••	••••	••••	•••∙	•••∙	∙∙∙∙		
Bar-tailed godwit C	••••	••••	••••	••••	∙∙∙∙	∙∙∙∙	∙∙∙∙	••••	••••	••••	••••	••••
Barn owl	••••	••••	••••	••••	••••	••••	••••	••••	••••	••••	••••	••••
Barnacle goose C	∙∙••	∙∙••	•••∙						∙∙∙•	••••	••••	••••
Black redstart	••••	••••	•••∙						∙∙∙•	••••	••••	••••
Black tern					••••			∙∙••	••∙∙			
Black-headed gull	••••	••••	••••	••••	••••	••••	••••	••••	••••	••••	••••	••••

	Jan	Feb	Mar	Apr	May	Jun	Jul	Aug	Sep	Oct	Nov	Dec
Black-tailed godwit C	••••	••••	••••	••••	•••∘		•∘∘∘	••••	••••	••••	••••	••••
Black-throated diver	•••∘	••••	••••	•∘∘∘					∘∘∘•	••••	••••	••••
Blackcap	∘∘∘∘	∘∘∘∘	∘∘∘∘	∘∘••	••••	•••	••••	••••	•••∘	∘∘∘∘	∘∘∘∘	∘∘∘∘
Blue tit	••••	••••	••••	••••	••••	•••	••••	••••	••••	••••	••••	••••
Brambling	••••	•••∘	•••∘	∘∘∘∘					∘∘∘•	••••	••••	••••
Brent goose C	••••	••••	•∘∘∘						∘∘∘•	••••	••••	
Bullfinch	••••	••••	••••	••••	••••	•••	••••	••••	••••	••••	••••	••••
Buzzard	••••	••••	••••	••••	••••	•••	••••	••••	••••	••••	••••	••••
Canada goose	••••	••••	••••	••••	••••	•••	••••	••••	••••	••••	••••	••••
Carrion crow	••••	••••	••••	••••	••••	•••	••••	••••	••••	••••	••••	••••
Chaffinch	••••	••••	••••	••••	••••	•••	••••	••••	••••	••••	••••	••••
Chiffchaff			∘∘∘•	••••	••••	•••	••••	••••	•••∘	∘∘∘∘	∘∘∘∘	∘∘∘∘
Coal tit	••••	••••	••••	••••	••••	•••	••••	••••	••••	••••	••••	••••
Collared dove	••••	••••	••••	••••	••••	•••	••••	••••	••••	••••	••••	••••
Common gull	••••	••••	••••	•••∘	∘∘∘∘	∘∘∘∘	∘∘∘∘	••••	••••	••••	••••	••••
Common sandpiper			∘∘∘∘	••••	••••	•••	••••	••••	••∘∘	∘∘∘∘		
Common scoter C	••••	••••	•••∘	∘∘∘∘			∘∘∘•	•••∘	••••	••••	•••∘	∘∘∘∘
Common tern				∘∘••	••••	•••	••••	••••	•••∘	∘∘∘		
Coot	••••	••••	••••	••••	••••	•••	••••	••••	••••	••••	••••	••••
Cormorant	••••	••••	••••	••••	••••	•••	••••	••••	••••	••••	••••	••••
Crossbill	••••	••••	••••	••••	••••	•••	••••	••••	••••	••••	••••	••••
Cuckoo				∘∘••	••••	•••	••••	••••	•••∘	∘∘∘∘		
Curlew	••••	••••	••••	••••	••••	•••	••••	••••	••••	••••	••••	••••
Curlew sandpiper				∘∘∘∘	∘∘∘∘		∘∘∘∘	•••∘	••••	••∘∘	∘∘∘∘	
Dipper	••••	••••	••••	••••	••••	•••	••••	••••	••••	••••	••••	••••
Dotterel				∘∘••	•••∘			∘∘∘•	•••∘	∘∘∘∘		
Dunlin		••••	••••	••••	••••	∘∘∘∘	∘∘∘∘	••••	••••	••••	••••	••••
Dunnock	••••	••••	••••	••••	••••	•••	••••	••••	••••	••••	••••	••••
Eider C	••••	••••	••••	••••	••••	•••	••••	••••	••••	••••	••••	•••∘
Feral pigeon	••••	••••	••••	••••	••••	•••	••••	••••	••••	••••	••••	••••
Fieldfare	••••	••••	•••∘	•••∘	∘∘				∘∘∘∘	••••	••••	••••
Fulmar C	∘∘∘∘	∘∘∘∘	∘∘∘∘	∘∘∘∘	∘∘∘∘	∘∘∘	∘∘∘∘	∘∘∘∘	∘∘∘∘	∘∘∘∘	∘∘∘∘	∘∘∘∘
Gannet C	∘∘∘∘	∘∘∘∘	∘∘∘∘	∘∘∘∘	∘∘∘∘	∘∘∘	∘∘∘∘	∘∘∘∘	∘∘∘∘	∘∘∘∘	∘∘∘∘	∘∘∘∘
Garden warbler				∘∘••	••••	•••	••••	••••	•••∘	∘∘∘∘		
Gargeney				∘∘∘∘	••••	∘∘∘∘		∘∘∘•	••∘∘			

	Jan	Feb	Mar	Apr	May	Jun	Jul	Aug	Sep	Oct	Nov	Dec
Glaucous gull	•	•	•							•	•	•
Goldcrest	•	•	•	•	•	•	•	•	•	•	•	•
Golden plover	•	•	•	•	•	•	•	•	•	•	•	•
Goldeneye	•	•	•	•	•				•	•	•	•
Goldfinch	•	•	•	•	•	•	•	•	•	•	•	•
Goosander	•	•	•	•	•	•	•	•	•	•	•	•
Goshawk	•	•	•	•	•	•	•	•	•	•	•	•
Grasshopper warbler				•	•	•	•	•	•			
Great black-backed gull	•	•	•	•	•	•	•	•	•	•	•	•
Great crested grebe	•	•	•	•	•	•	•	•	•	•	•	•
Great skua			•	•			•	•				
Great spotted woodpecker	•	•	•	•	•	•	•	•	•	•	•	•
Great tit	•	•	•	•	•	•	•	•	•	•	•	•
Green sandpiper	•	•	•	•	•			•	•	•	•	•
Green woodpecker	•	•	•	•	•	•	•	•	•	•	•	•
Greenfinch	•	•	•	•	•	•	•	•	•	•	•	•
Greenshank	•	•	•	•	•	•	•	•	•	•	•	•
Grey heron	•	•	•	•	•	•	•	•	•	•	•	•
Grey partridge	•	•	•	•	•	•	•	•	•	•	•	•
Grey plover C	•	•	•	•	•	•	•	•	•	•	•	•
Grey wagtail	•	•	•	•	•	•	•	•	•	•	•	•
Greylag goose	•	•	•	•	•	•	•	•	•	•	•	•
Guillemot C	•	•	•	•	•	•	•	•	•	•	•	•
Hawfinch	•	•	•	•	•	•	•	•	•	•	•	•
Hen harrier	•	•	•	•	•	•	•	•	•	•	•	•
Herring gull	•	•	•	•	•	•	•	•	•	•	•	•
Hobby					•	•	•	•				
House martin				•	•	•	•	•	•	•		
House sparrow	•	•	•	•	•	•	•	•	•	•	•	•
Jack snipe	•	•	•	•					•	•	•	•
Jackdaw	•	•	•	•	•	•	•	•	•	•	•	•
Jay	•	•	•	•	•	•	•	•	•	•	•	•
Kestrel	•	•	•	•	•	•	•	•	•	•	•	•
Kingfisher	•	•	•	•	•	•	•	•	•	•	•	•

	Jan	Feb	Mar	Apr	May	Jun	Jul	Aug	Sep	Oct	Nov	Dec
Kittiwake	••••	••••	••••	••••	••••	••••	••••	••••	••••	••••	••••	••••
Knot C	••••	••••	••••	••••	••••	••••	••••	••••	••••	••••	••••	••••
Lapwing	••••	••••	••••	••••	••••	••••	••••	••••	••••	••••	••••	••••
Leach's petrel								••••	••••	••••		
Lesser black-backed gull	••••	••••	••••	••••	••••	••••	••••	••••	••••	••••	••••	••••
Lesser spotted woodpecker	••••	••••	••••	••••	••••	••••	••••	••••	••••	••••	••••	••••
Lesser whitethroat			••	••••	••••	••••	••••	••••	•••			
Linnet	••••	••••	••••	••••	••••	••••	••••	••••	••••	••••	••••	••••
Little grebe	••••	••••	••••	••••	••••	••••	••••	••••	••••	••••	••••	••••
Little gull	••••	••••	••••	••••	••••	••••	••••	••••	••••	••••	••••	••••
Little owl	••••	••••	••••	••••	••••	••••	••••	••••	••••	••••	••••	••••
Little ringed plover				••••	••••	••••	••••	••••	••••	•••		
Little stint C				••••	•••			•••	••••	•••		
Little tern C			••••	•••			•••	••••	•••			
Long-eared owl	••••	••••	••••	••••	••••	••••	••••	••••	••••	••••	••••	••••
Long-tailed tit	••••	••••	••••	••••	••••	••••	••••	••••	••••	••••	••••	••••
Mallard	••••	••••	••••	••••	••••	••••	••••	••••	••••	••••	••••	••••
Manx shearwater C			••••	••••	••••	••••	••••	••				
Marsh harrier			••••	••			••••	••				
Marsh tit	••••	••••	••••	••••	••••	••••	••••	••••	••••	••••	••••	••••
Meadow pipit	••••	••••	••••	••••	••••	••••	••••	••••	••••	••••	••••	••••
Mediterranean gull	••••	••••	••••	••••	••••	••••	••••	••••	••••	••••	••••	••••
Merlin	••••	••••	••••	••••	••••	••••	••••	••••	••••	••••	••••	••••
Mistle thrush	••••	••••	••••	••••	••••	••••	••••	••••	••••	••••	••••	••••
Moorhen	••••	••••	••••	••••	••••	••••	••••	••••	••••	••••	••••	••••
Mute swan	••••	••••	••••	••••	••••	••••	••••	••••	••••	••••	••••	••••
Nuthatch	••••	••••	••••	••••	••••	••••	••••	••••	••••	••••	••••	••••
Osprey			••••	••••	••••	••••	••••	••••	••••			
Oystercatcher	••••	••••	••••	••••	••••	••••	••••	••••	••••	••••	••••	••••
Peregrine	••••	••••	••••	••••	••••	••••	••••	••••	••••	••••	••••	••••
Pheasant	••••	••••	••••	••••	••••	••••	••••	••••	••••	••••	••••	••••
Pied flycatcher			••••	••••	••••	••••	••••	•••	••••			
Pied wagtail	••••	••••	••••	••••	••••	••••	••••	••••	••••	••••	••••	••••
Pink-footed goose C	••••	••••	••••	••••	••••	••••	••••	••••	••••	••••	••••	••••

	Jan	Feb	Mar	Apr	May	Jun	Jul	Aug	Sep	Oct	Nov	Dec
Pintail	••••	••••	••••	••••	◦◦◦		◦◦◦	◦◦◦	••••	••••	••••	••••
Pochard	••••	••••	••••	••••	••••	••••	••••	••••	••••	••••	••••	••••
Quail					◦◦◦◦	◦◦						
Raven	••••	••••	••••	••••	••••	••••	••••	••••	••••	••••	••••	••••
Red grouse	••••	••••	••••	••••	••••	••••	••••	••••	••••	••••	••••	••••
Red-breasted merganser	••••	••••	••••	••••	••••	••••	••••	••••	••••	••••	••••	••••
Red-legged partridge	••••	••••	••••	••••	••••	••••	••••	••••	••••	••••	••••	••••
Red-throated diver C	◦◦◦◦	◦◦◦◦	◦◦◦◦	◦◦◦◦					◦◦◦◦	◦◦◦◦	◦◦◦◦	◦◦◦◦
Redpoll	••••	••••	••••	••••	••••	••••	••••	••••	••••	••••	••••	••••
Redshank	••••	••••	••••	••••	••••	••••	••••	••••	••••	••••	••••	••••
Redstart				◦◦◦•	••••	••••	••••	••••	◦◦◦◦			
Redwing	••••	••••	••••	••••	◦◦◦◦				◦◦◦•	••••	••••	••••
Reed bunting	••••	••••	••••	••••	••••	••••	••••	••••	••••	••••	••••	••••
Ring ouzel			◦◦◦•	••••	••••	••••	••••	••••	◦◦◦◦	◦◦◦◦		
Ringed plover	••••	••••	••••	••••	••••	••••	••••	••••	••••	••••	••••	••••
Robin	••••	••••	••••	••••	••••	••••	••••	••••	••••	••••	••••	••••
Rock pipit C	◦◦◦◦	◦◦◦◦	◦◦◦◦	◦◦◦◦						◦◦◦◦	••••	••••
Rook	••••	••••	••••	••••	••••	••••	••••	••••	••••	••••	••••	••••
Ruddy duck	••••	••••	••••	••••	••••	••••	••••	••••	••••	••••	••••	••••
Ruff			◦◦◦◦	••••	◦◦◦◦		◦◦◦◦	••••	◦◦◦◦			
Sand martin			◦◦••	••••	••••	••••	••••	••••	◦◦◦◦			
Sanderling C	••••	••••	••••	◦◦◦•	◦◦◦◦			◦◦◦◦	••••	••••	••••	••••
Sandwich tern C			◦◦••	••••	••••	••••	••••	••••	◦◦			
Scaup	◦◦◦◦	◦◦◦◦	◦◦							◦◦◦◦	••••	••••
Sedge warbler				◦◦◦◦	••••	••••	••••	••••	◦◦◦◦			
Shelduck	••••	••••	••••	••••	••••	••••	••••	••••	••••	••••	••••	••••
Short-eared owl	••••	••••	••••	••••	••••	••••	••••	••••	••••	••••	••••	••••
Shoveler	••••	••••	••••	••••	◦◦◦◦	◦◦◦	••••	••••	••••	••••	••••	••••
Siskin	••••	••••	••••	••••	••••	••••	••••	••••	••••	••••	••••	••••
Skylark	••••	••••	••••	••••	••••	••••	••••	••••	••••	••••	••••	••••
Slavonian grebe C	◦◦◦◦	◦◦◦◦	◦◦◦							◦◦◦◦	••••	••••
Snipe	••••	••••	••••	••••	••••	••••	••••	••••	••••	••••	••••	••••
Snow bunting	◦◦◦◦	◦◦◦◦	◦◦◦							◦◦◦◦	◦◦◦◦	◦◦◦◦
Song thrush	••••	••••	••••	••••	••••	••••	••••	••••	••••	••••	••••	••••
Sparrow hawk	••••	••••	••••	••••	••••	••••	••••	••••	••••	••••	••••	••••

	Jan	Feb	Mar	Apr	May	Jun	Jul	Aug	Sep	Oct	Nov	Dec
Spotted flycatcher				···•	••••	••••	••••	••••	••••	····		
Stock dove	••••	••••	••••	••••	••••	••••	••••	••••	••••	••••	••••	••••
Stonechat	••••	••••	••••	••••	••••	••••	••••	••••	••••	••••	••••	••••
Swallow				···•	••••	••••	••••	••••	••••	••••	····	
Swift				··••	••••	••••	••••	····	··			
Tawny owl	••••	••••	••••	••••	••••	••••	••••	••••	••••	••••	••••	••••
Teal	••••	••••	••••	••••	••••	••••	••••	••••	••••	••••	••••	••••
Tree pipit				···•	••••	••••	••••	••••	••••	····		
Tree sparrow	••••	••••	••••	••••	••••	••••	••••	••••	••••	••••	••••	••••
Tree creeper	••••	••••	••••	••••	••••	••••	••••	••••	••••	••••	••••	••••
Tufted duck	••••	••••	••••	••••	••••	••••	••••	••••	••••	••••	••••	••••
Turnstone C	••••	••••	••••	••••	••••	••••	····	••••	••••	••••	••••	••••
Twite	••••	••••	••••	····	····	····	····	····	••••	••••	••••	••••
Water rail	····	····	····	····	····	····	····	····	····	····	····	····
Waxwing	····	····	····							····	····	····
Wheatear			····	••••	••••	••••	••••	••••	••••	····		
Whimbrel				···••	••··			••••	····	····		
Whinchat				···•	••••	••••	••••	••••	··••	····		
Whitethroat				···•	••••	••••	••••	••••	••••	····		
Whooper swan	••••	••••	••••	····	····	····	····	····	••••	••••	••••	••••
Wigeon	••••	••••	••••	••••	··	····	····	····	••••	••••	••••	••••
Willow warbler				·•••	••••	••••	••••	••••	····			
Wood sandpiper				·•··			••••	····				
Wood warbler				····	••••	••••	••••	····				
Woodcock	••••	••••	••••	••••	••••	••••	••••	••••	••••	••••	••••	••••
Wren	••••	••••	••••	••••	••••	••••	••••	••••	••••	••••	••••	••••
Yellow wagtail				···•	••••	••••	••••	••••	····			
Yellow hammer	••••	••••	••••	••••	••••	••••	••••	••••	••••	••••	••••	••••

Further reading

Birds of Lancashire, Mitchell, 1892.

Birds of Lancashire, Oakes, 1953

The Status and Distribution of Birds in Lancashire, Spencer, 1975

The Atlas of Breeding Birds of Lancashire and North Merseyside 2001, Pyefinch & Golbourn

Birdwatching/Walking Notes

Birdwatching/Walking Notes

Birdwatching/Walking Notes

Birdwatching/Walking Notes

Birdwatching/Walking Notes

Birdwatching/Walking Notes

Birdwatching/Walking Notes

Birdwatching/Walking Notes

Birdwatching/Walking Notes

Birdwatching/Walking Notes